My Asakusa

My Asakusa

COMING OF AGE IN PRE-WAR TOKYO

by
Sadako Sawamura

Translated by
Norman E. Stafford
and
Yasuhiro Kawamura

Tuttle Publishing
Boston • Rutland, Vermont • Tokyo

First published in 2000 by Tuttle Publishing, an imprint of Periplus
Editions (HK) Ltd, with editorial offices at 153 Milk Street,
Boston, Massachusetts 02109.

©2000 by Charles E. Tuttle Publishing Co., Inc.

ISBN 0-8048-2135-6

Distributed by

USA
Tuttle Publishing
Distribution Center
Airport Industrial Park
364 Innovation Drive
North Clarendon, VT 05759-9436
Tel: (802) 773-8930
Tel: (800) 526-2778

JAPAN
Tuttle Publishing
RK Building, 2nd Floor
2-13-10 Shimo-Meguro,
Meguro-Ku
Tokyo 153 0064
Tel: (03) 5437-0171
Fax: (03) 5437-0755

CANADA
Raincoast Books
8680 Cambie Street
Vancouver, British Columbia
V6P 6M9
Tel: (604) 323-7100
Fax: (604) 323-2600

SOUTHEAST ASIA
Berkeley Books Pte Ltd
5 Little Road #08-01
Singapore 536983
Tel: (65) 280-1330
Fax: (65) 280-6290

First edition
06 05 04 03 02 01 00   10 9 8 7 6 5 4 3 2 1

Printed in the United States of America

✦ *Table of Contents* ✦

6 ♦ *Table of Contents*

✦ *Introduction* ✦

SADAKO SAWAMURA DIED ON AUGUST 16, 1996, AT the age of 87. The former actress and author of books was a popular figure in Japan and the subject of numerous television interviews and news stories. After a career in theater, motion pictures, and television that spanned more than half a century, Sawamura remained both charming and elegant. Although physically frail in the last decade of her life, she maintained the strong beliefs acquired in her youth and expressed them vigorously and precisely, revealing a mind as acute as it was in her prime. Sadako Sawamura was a fascinating woman, and the story of her life resonates for Japanese readers of pre- and post-war generations.

Early in her career Sawamura specialized in character parts. In 1956 she won the Joyu-Joen-Sho, the distinguished supporting actress award, at the eleventh Mainichi Eiga Concours, an acknowledgment of her performance in several films. The first of her books, *Kai-no-uta* [The Song of a Shell], published in 1969, recalls her late adolescence and early adulthood and was produced in 1978 as a play for NHK, Japanese Public Television. *My Asakusa* [pronouced "Ah sock sah"] (1976), Sawamura's second book, won the 1977 Japan

Essayists' Club Prize. Because it recounts her earliest years, *My Asakusa* offers the greatest insight of any of her books into the influences that formed her character.

Perhaps "character" is the key word in describing her, because, for the Japanese, Sadako Sawamura is more than simply a beloved actress. She was a woman with traditional values who adapted to and flourished in the modern world. Hers is a success story—representative of many Japanese who were born into a traditional culture, suffered through the most destructive period in the nation's history, and thrived in a changing world. Her life is both a reminder of the past and a model for the future.

My Asakusa dramatizes the values that enabled Sadako Sawamura and her country to achieve that success. The wide-ranging essays, in loose chronological order, create a montage of the world that shaped her personality—her family, the Asakusa district of Tokyo, the Senso-ji temple, the Miyato Theater, the small shops and narrow streets, and the minor players in the drama—the shopkeepers, theater people, geisha, friends, and neighbors.

The physical setting in which Sawamura spent her last years best symbolizes the extent of her success and the position she occupied in the minds of the Japanese people. Her apartment was on an upper floor of a modern high-rise building near Kamakura, a lovely and historically significant ocean-side city. The furnishings combined contemporary Western with traditional Japanese. Through the glass doors that dominate one wall is a spectacular view of the Pacific Ocean with a shrine in the foreground. From the sheltered balcony,

Sawamura, arrayed in kimono and *obi,* could direct the attention of her guests to the lovely hills of the Izu Peninsula, beyond which lies the sacred Mount Fuji.

This home was far different than that of Sawamura's youth. Asakusa, where she was born on November 11, 1908, is in a low section of Tokyo. The narrow, noisy streets are crowded with rows of houses and shops. Although her family was not poor, Sawamura had few material advantages, and her success was the result of her own effort. She gained admission to a prestigious high school, meeting her expenses by tutoring young children. She received little encouragement from her parents and others who believed that girls needed only minimal formal education, and was ridiculed by her peers who disparaged her social status.

Nevertheless, Sawamura graduated and was admitted to what is now Nihon Women's University to prepare for a teaching degree. But events of the day caught her. The social and political unrest in Japan offended her sensibilities, and her compassion for the poor led her to support socialist causes, ironically introducing her to acting. She joined a left-wing theater group. When university officials learned of her affiliation, she was forced to choose between withdrawing from the theater troupe or from the university. Three months before graduation, she left the university.

Sawamura joined the Communist Youth League to continue working for the poor and, at age twenty-two, married one of its leaders, Shigeo Imamura. In the 1920s right-wing militarists had gained control in Japan, and the Communist Party was outlawed. Sawamura, arrested for her membership in the Youth

League, refused to renounce her beliefs and instead affirmed her support for the workers even if released. She was detained for over a year and spent ten months of that time in an isolated cell. She was granted bail on condition that she divorce Imamura. She nevertheless resumed working with him, this time underground. When he was arrested, he betrayed her. Imprisoned and tortured, disillusioned with her ex-husband and the revolutionary movement and facing a three-year prison sentence, Sawamura left him and renounced her commitment to the Communists in exchange for five years probation. Sawamura then seriously pursued a career in films. After several years, she met her future husband Yasuhiko Ohashi, a critic of the arts and publisher of an arts magazine, *Eiga Geijutsu* [Cinema Art], with whom she would share a happy and rewarding life until his death in 1994. But she remained committed to the principle of respect for all people and to supporting a government that assures their freedom.

Sawamura achieved a position few Japanese of her gender and background ever reach. In her mature years her world was spacious, financially secure, and modern, yet rooted in tradition. She lived in the present serenely without fear of the future. She was above the din of everyday life, in one of the more desirable locations in Japan. While in fact only seventy kilometers from her birthplace in Tokyo, she was figuratively much further from Asakusa than is apparent to most Westerners and perhaps to many younger Japanese.

The distance she had come must be measured against the class system on which her society was based, remnants of which remain. Asakusa lies in the center of the

Shitamachi district of Tokyo. Sometimes translated as "downtown," Shitamachi is much more than a business district. Arising at the beginning of the Edo period (1603–1868), Shitamachi was a means of segregating the service class—craftspeople, small shopkeepers, merchants, and manufacturers—from the upper classes. The area contrasts to the *yamanote* [literally the "hills" or "bluffs"] district of the *samurai* class and presently of white-collar and upper-middle-class families.

In the late Edo period, Asakusa and the contiguous entertainment district, Yoshiwara, prospered, and its inhabitants developed strong cultural identity and pride in their way of life. In time, an exciting artistic subculture emerged in Tokyo's Shitamachi. The Kabuki theater, the geisha quarters, puppet theaters with *shamisen* music, and similar entertainment all contributed to Shitamachi's vitality. While the "pleasure quarters" image of Asakusa heightened its attraction to visitors, it also created an aura of the risqué and the base. Residents of Asakusa, though, saw the various enterprises of the area—both business and entertainment—as virtues. Asakusa was a challenging environment in which to live, but the challenges created strength of character and a sense of belonging as well. Thus, when Sawamura refers to herself as an "Asakusa girl," she is saying much more than merely identifying where she spent her girlhood. The area supported her as she "came of age"—whether learning the fundamentals of applying makeup or the consequences of depending on a man.

Shitamachi culture, however, was not the only intellectual influence on area residents. Its rival was the Senso-ji temple. Founded in 628 A.C.E., Senso-ji is one of the oldest temples in Tokyo and is central to both the spiritual and economic health of the community. The various buildings and statuary on its extensive grounds are physical reminders to the people of Asakusa of their long cultural history—both Buddhist and Shinto.

Although in Japan, *temple* usually refers to the grounds, buildings, and icons of a Buddhist facility and *shrine* to those of Shinto, that is not the case at Senso-ji. Despite the forced separation of Buddhism and Shinto during the Meiji Restoration, Senso-ji is the site of important symbols of both of Japan's major religions. The fame of the Asakusa Shrine may even rival that of the dominant feature of the temple, Buddhism's Bodhisattva Kannon. The Senso-ji is a fitting daily reminder to the people of Asakusa of just who they are and what they have been.

Sawamura never explicitly alludes to Kannon in *My Asakusa,* but the deity may have been more important to her work than even she realizes. As a savior with "boundless compassion for suffering humanity," the goddess is "one of the most important and beloved deities in popular Japanese Buddhism,"[1] as well as one of Asakusa's major attractions and a source of pride for all Japanese. Compassion is one of the most cherished values emerging from *My Asakusa.* Essays frequently focus on a character's sympathetic nature or lack of it. Some of the most moving moments in these portraits are of the kindness of Sawamura's mother or of her father's insensitivity.

---

[1]Paul Waley, *Tokyo Now & Then: An Explorer's Guide* (New York: Weatherhill, 1984), p. 190.

However, Senso-ji is more than a physical reminder or symbolic device. It is the actual setting for several incidents, and its many celebrations and festivals—with fireworks and parades, crowds of vendors, actors, geisha, housewives, and excited children—provide the backdrop for others. The temple serves a social, more than a religious, function for Asakusa residents and its numberless visitors. For although many Japanese, including Sawamura, deny that they are religious, these same people usually observe the rituals of Buddhism and Shintoism. They celebrate the holidays and festivals while paying little attention to, if not actually ignoring, the more religious elements. In *My Asakusa* the preparation for such events, or the aftermath, is often as important as the event itself.

Where people gather for social purposes, business interests also thrive. Just as today, a major attraction of Senso-ji in Sawamura's childhood was shopping among the numerous small stores filling the grounds of the temple and catering to the needs of visitors and locals. On special occasions, vendors from outside the district hawked their wares, and temporary shops opened to serve the crowds. In a much greater sense than is true of their Western counterparts, the areas surrounding temples and shrines were exciting commercial enterprises. Local residents were also more than consumers: They operated the shops, food stands, restaurants, and stalls selling crafts and trinkets. Their livelihood depended on activity generated by the temple.

While Kabuki and the Miyato Theater are part of the unique atmosphere of Asakusa, they also play a significant role in the life of Sawamura and her family. Her father was manager of a troupe that performed at the Miyato Theater, nationally famous for its style and quality of Kabuki. His ambition for his sons—to become Kabuki actors—was one he had aspired to himself at one time, and the boys were apprenticed in the theater at an early age. This ambition, in part, explains the careful attention the father gave his sons at the expense of his wife and daughters.

Westerners might well compare the Japanese attitude toward Kabuki to the attitude of the English-speaking world toward Shakespearean theater. In both traditions today the plays are regarded as models of literary excellence, yet the average person has little actual knowledge of more than a few of them.

Like Shakespearean theater, Kabuki has not always enjoyed unalloyed admiration. When it began in the seventeenth century, Kabuki consisted of simple variety shows performed by wandering troupes of female entertainers. But because they often engaged in sensuous dances or supplemented their income by prostitution, female performers were prohibited in 1629. However, the male replacements engaged in similar activities, and for a time Kabuki was banned entirely. When it was restored, both the performers and the plays were more respectable than before. Kabuki increased in complexity, acquiring many conventions and highly stylized acting.

Families of Kabuki actors developed. In time, these families dominated, and gaining access to the profession became difficult for outsiders. Sometimes the families apprenticed non-family members who then assumed the family name. Meritorious actors sometimes were permitted to take the name of a prestigious family.

Originally, Sawamura's family name was Kato, but when her older brother Tomokazu was apprenticed to the famous actor Sojuro Sawamura VII (1875–1949), he assumed the name Kunitaro Sawamura. Sojuro Sawamura was regarded as the last of the great Kabuki actors to embrace a particular acting style from the Edo period, and the family name carried great weight. This honor may be little understood by English-speaking readers. In the egalitarianism of the late twentieth century, given names often take precedence over family names, and reliance on ancestral ties for respect and identity seems both archaic and undemocratic. Consequently, changing *Kato* to *Sawamura* might appear to be no more than assuming a stage name. For the Japanese, however, the name "Sawamura" resonates from the golden age of Kabuki.

Nonetheless, Kato's sons were not destined for success in Kabuki. Despite his earning a prestigious name, Kunitaro Sawamura's lack of biological lineage in this virtual caste system prevented him from obtaining major roles. He then entered films. As a child, Sawamura's younger brother, Tokunosuke Kato, was a skilled Kabuki actor. But he never advanced enough to take a famous Kabuki family name. Rather he became a well-known actor in other venues.

The tradition of assuming the name of a prestigious acting family is the most significant reason that Teiko Kato became "Sadako Sawamura." When she became a film actress, Teiko Kato was allowed to use the family name Sawamura. In kanji, the Chinese form of writing widely used in Japanese writing, "Teiko" and "Sadako" are written identically, but can be pronounced differently. At the urging of the president of Nikkatsu Movie Company, Teiko took the name Sadako to sound more formal. In Japanese, "-ko" is a female suffix. (The suffix "-bo," as in "Tei-bo" is a form of endearment used in both female and male names, and this form of the author's name occurs often in the book.)

While still appealing today, Kabuki was wildly popular when Sawamura's father, Dentaro Kato, was a child. As an art form, Kabuki reached its peak in the nineteenth century, and it captured the young boy's imagination. He may well have had reason to seek such an escape. Dentaro was born in 1868, the beginning of the Meiji Restoration, and the ferment of the time directly affected his life. His father was a man of means, but because of alliances in his mother's family with a faction of the Mito clan, a rival group broke into his father's businesses and robbed them. This loss led to the fall of the house and the family fortune. Soon after, Dentaro's father died. His mother, in reduced circumstances, took him and his younger sister to Asakusa, establishing the ties to place which his daughter would later feel so deeply.

For a time, Dentaro was apprenticed to a pawnshop owner, but, surrounded by the many theater people in the area, he told his mother of his desire to be an actor. Despite the elevated status of Kabuki, actors had poor reputations, especially in the eyes of a fallen *samurai* family. Over the objection of an uncle, a compromise was struck, and Dentaro was apprenticed to a playwright, a position of higher social status, but one for which Dentaro apparently had little talent or enthusiasm. In his lifetime, he wrote only one play that was performed. Later he would say that he was too popular with women to find time to write a script.

Despite the intended humor, Dentaro's rationalization reflected some truth, and his flirtations and infidelities after his marriage caused his wife and daughter great pain. He married late in life, at age thirty-five, and some patterns of his behavior were probably more suited to a bachelor than to a husband and father. Like many of his time, he wished to have a family, in particular, sons who would be actors. As in many countries, the contributions of most women in nineteenth-century Japan were undervalued and their prospects limited. So Dentaro Kato's giving his first daughter to his childless sister for adoption was not extraordinary. It does suggest, however, the extent to which his sons occupied his attention.

The wife he chose, Matsu, was twenty-five at the time of their marriage and fulfilled Dentaro's three conditions for a wife: 1) good health, for bearing his sons; 2) a sharp mind, so the children would have no trouble learning their lines; 3) and good housekeeping skills. Matsu more than fulfilled the conditions. Perhaps her intelligence exacerbated the grief she later experienced with her husband. Her father was a *samurai,* and like many others in his position during the early years of the Meiji Restoration, with little experience in conducting business, he lost money. Her parents intentionally denied Matsu a formal education because they feared that she was too intelligent and schooling would prevent her from finding a proper match. She was also a plain woman with a round face and dark complexion—characteristics that made her common by her husband's standards.

Dentaro Kato may have used his wife's physical features to rationalize his infidelity, but his comments about them in one instance permanently altered his married life for the worse. His second son, Tokunosuke, resembled his mother, leading Kato to say that the child was not his. His words cut so deeply that his wife never again shared his bed. Sawamura recalls that her mother always slept downstairs with Tokunosuke and her while her father slept upstairs with his older son, Tomokazu.

Many essays in *My Asakusa* reveal Sawamura's ambivalent feelings toward her father, and her responses to his complex personality are compelling. She sees him as the head of the family, as the one who usually gets his way—in most instances a very strong man. He is also a good provider who cares for his family. He works steadily and is not physically abusive. His children have a happy life and respect their father. In many ways he seems superior to other men of Asakusa. However, he is also egocentric, vain, and pampered. Although he promotes his sons to the exclusion of his daughter, his most egregious insensitivity is to his wife. Of course, men of the day, West and East, enjoyed the privileges of the day. But Kato often went beyond what was acceptable at that time and in that place. The unhappiness and frustrations he experienced as a child and young man may explain, if not justify, his behavior.

However conflicted her feelings were toward her father, Sawamura's feelings toward her mother are admiring and loving. Matsu is the most engaging figure in *My Asakusa* and was the strongest positive influence on her daughter, endowing her with sufficient qualities of character with which to combat the institutionalized sexism which she faced. Devoted to her family and concerned for others, she is portrayed as a person of action. Matsu never demands tasks of her daughter that she herself would not do; she shows her how to cook, sew, and deal with others fairly and sympathetically. Her wisdom is apparent in their many conversations. Matsu is never condescending, and her observations are all the more penetrating because she reveals her feelings infrequently. She knows when to speak and when to be silent. Her ability to deal with her husband reveals her great strength of character. "Mother's *Marumage* Hairstyle" may well be the most moving essay of the collection, and readers can imagine the depths of her pain. Like her mother, Sawamura knows when to say nothing.

As she implies in the Author's Note, Sawamura is aware that her retrospective account is a success story. Asakusa is the locale, and each incident enlarges the reader's understanding of the influences that made her the person she later became. Her memoirs, especially because of its essay form, possess a quality shared by all writers of autobiography: selectivity in the events recounted and their descriptions. Selectivity is not a limitation—all autobiographers have *a priori* purposes, acknowledged or not. What is omitted is often more revealing than what is included. Historians may differ with Sawamura's interpretation of "facts," and participants in the incidents may interpret events differently. But the details Sadako Sawamura chooses to reveal, as well as those she does not include, provide a subtle portrait of the places, people, events, and ideas of the Tokyo of her youth.

Sawamura attributes her "character as a Shitamachi woman" to her "experiences on the back alleys" (Author's Note). This Asakusa was stimulating for a young girl but not idyllic. The numerous festivals around the Senso-ji are a happy backdrop for poignant and sometimes tragic events. Behind the action on center stage—whether as trivial as a shopkeeper's welcome to gawking but penniless children or as momentous as her mother's change of hairstyle because "its role [was] over"—Sawamura portrays an essentially cheerful community supported by a common spiritual foundation. The opening essay, "Special Fruit," illustrates the sense of community that pervades her book. A produce vendor's wife tells Teiko of special tangerines suitable for the young girl's family. The fruit was inexpensive because it was slightly spoiled. Yet Teiko's mother was happy to receive it. In commenting on the transaction, the author attributes a noble motive to the shopkeeper and a grateful attitude to her mother.

But Sawamura is not naive. Other essays disclose deficiencies in character (even in the fullest of her portraits, her mother), selfishness, and ignorance. But when given a choice of motivation or attitude, she invariably chooses the positive alternative. Although Shitamachi life may actually have been a bitter struggle for many, Sawamura's vision of her formative years is emotionally healthy and satisfying. She recognizes ugliness when she meets it but places it in a larger perspective, one that delights in the beauty of a great performance while acknowledging the occasional flaw.

Sawamura's surroundings gave her several opportunities to choose the darker options. Although her brothers took advantage of their status in a male-dominated society, her relationship with them reflects the happy family life she enjoyed. But her sister offers a stark reminder that Sadako Sawamura's life could have been quite different. Her sister is mentioned casually twice in the book. In the Author's Note, Sawamura thanks her sister for her help in recalling incidents. In "The *Nigenkin* and the Belle of Nakamise," she mentions that her sister had been adopted by their aunt. *My Asakusa* does not explain the circumstances of this adoption, and exploring them here is inappropriate. The practice of adoption, so that a child could be of help to the adoptive family, was common in Japan in the past. This minor feature of the book reveals how tenuous Sawamura's life could have been.

The precarious existence of young women in the area is illustrated by the several stories containing characters who live in the Yoshiwara district, the gay quarters adjoining Asakusa, which housed geisha, courtesans, and prostitutes, offering countless instances of the worst of human behavior. "The Girl from Akita" is the story of a young woman who cherishes the impossible hope of removing herself from a life where she is treated like a "dog." In "The Platinum *Koi* Ring," Sawamura's brother has an affair with a courtesan and then ignores her. The problem is resolved with the woman's probable death in the Great Kanto Earthquake of 1923, a resolution which underscores her brother's culpability. The fact that Sawamura remembers such incidents, portrays them vividly, and suffers when they affect those dearest to her indicates their powerful influence.

Some women triumph magnificently over their hardships, as in "The Tale of the Manseian Noodle Shop," the longest essay in the collection. Other stories of women are implicitly juxtaposed to Sawamura's own achievements. Although these women are successful, their goals are frequently limited, suggesting the lack of available opportunity.

Other essays recount failures, not only women's, but also men's. Some, like the "Cherry-Blossom Actor," are humorous. A shy man by nature, he could perform well only when drunk. His is a comic tale because he was not unhappy, but his story comments on the problems actors faced. Her own vulnerability is implied in "Crazy About Acting," where Sawamura sympathetically describes the struggles of her younger brother, who she believed was a man of great but unfulfilled talent.

Sawamura's portrait of the place, its people, times, and mores, gives substance to values which, even today, hold a special place for many Japanese. These values transcend time and nationality and create the universal charm of *My Asakusa*. These are the same values that formed a character strong enough to endure and overcome personal and national hardships and that compelled the author to refer to herself even in later life as an "Asakusa girl."

—Norman E. Stafford

✦ *Foreword* ✦

SAWAMURA-SAN'S BOOKS OF ESSAYS ARE ALL WON-
derful, but the best is *My Asakusa [Watashi no
Asakusa]*. I believe *My Asakusa* and *The Song of a
Shell [Kai-no-Uta]*, the account of the first half of her
life, are Sawamura-san's masterpieces. Every time I read
My Asakusa, I am amazed that the days of a certain period, in one particular locality, have been recorded in a
style so proper to the subject. Undoubtedly, the virtues
of the book derive from Sawamura-san's ability, but as I
read on, I thought that something like "the soul of the
time and the place" (perhaps I am being too formal in
applying such terms to Asakusa) had given her a helping
hand behind the scenes. I feel this way because a sense
of happiness and serenity always flows beneath these
reminiscences.

In the Postscript of *The Song of a Shell* Sawamura-san
says, "It is amazing how many things I still remember.
The things I thought I had long forgotten kept coming
to my mind. It is as though they had been biding their
time, heaped one upon another without stirring, holding
their breath, at the bottom of my tightly-locked mind."
This comment is more suited to *My Asakusa*. "Special

Fruit," "The Sanja Festival," "My Red-Thonged *Hiyori,*" and "The Sap of the Sponge Gourd" had all been "biding their time, heaped one upon another without stirring, holding their breath" for her to recall. Sawamura-san thinks fondly of each memory, cherishes them all, and is pleased that they have made her what she is. She writes with pride: "Wherever I live in Tokyo, I am an Asakusa girl. My character was nurtured by my experiences on the back alleys of Asakusa." Her remark sounds commonplace, but may I ask how many of us can look back on our childhood with Sawamura-san's sense of security? I was born in Senzoku-machi, Asakusa, her hometown, twenty-six years later than she. Her Asakusa was about that of the Taisho period [1912–1926], and mine is the first ten years of the Showa era [1926–1989]. "The Hozuki Fair," "*Tanka-bai:* A Crude Language Sale," "*Hatsumode*, the First Visit to the Temple on New Year's Day," and the custom of throwing decayed teeth that had come out (an upper tooth under the porch and a lower tooth on the roof)—I can recall each of these. Yet in my time the people around me directed their attention elsewhere. The upheavals of those days, exemplified by the China-Japan War [1937–1941] and the Second World War, deprived us of the composure of mind necessary to cherish daily life in Asakusa.

Reading her book, we appreciate the life the wars overturned, though we believe the wars alone did not change the life described there. Not only did the shortage of food in the postwar days upset this world, but so did economic growth, democracy, the reliance on science and rationalism that followed. These factors changed a world in which lived many old customs, small illogical wishes, an aesthetic sense incompatible with the spirit of equality of the sexes, and counting-out rhymes—and we did not regret the loss!

We cannot say these changes are all wrong. Here lies the source of the difficulty and of the poverty of our modern lives. In Sawamura-san's Asakusa, we might accept our neighbors' counsel, "You must endure your husband's flirtations"; however, after the war, we would have rejected such advice. The soundness of the dinner table at which father alone ate *sashimi* and the rest of the family had to be content with seasoned potatoes has been questioned in Japanese families these forty years. And we now live in a time when we cannot allow ourselves to say imprudently, "You are only a girl. Stop complaining."

We cannot with any justice lament these changes. Clearly we have overcome many of the inconveniences, inequalities, and fallacies of the Taisho period. Logically we should be living in a better age than before. But on reading this book, I perceive that the world that nurtured the young Sawamura-san had more spiritual richness than our world, and we feel that our world, rough and loose, lacks sweetness and taste. Why? Perhaps just as the dead are visualized with more graceful and clearer images than the living, so the world of memory is cleaner and sweeter than the contemporary world. Then does it follow that whoever looks back on childhood and adolescence can recall a charming world like that of *My Asakusa*? No, I don't think so. The charm of her world is not attributed solely to her excellent writing. Her world makes me realize how greatly the times have changed:

February 8 is the day for the Memorial Service for Needles. Together Asakusa women visit the Awashima Myojin in the precincts of the Kannon temple [the Senso-ji]. Awashima-sama is a deity of sewing. In those days sewing was the most important skill required of Shitamachi girls. "If you are a poor seamstress, your husband and children will go in rags. It's a discredit on a woman," my mother used to say.

So writes Sawamura-san.

What equanimity! Although our modern age has many advantages, to a frightening degree we have lost this balance. We are, in our daily consciousness, more rational. In her time, if women were told that their lack of sewing skills would shame them, they strenuously sought to improve and would visit the Myojin-sama as a group on the day of the Memorial Service for Needles. For better or worse, we have become estranged from this way of living.

Mass media constantly intrude on our daily lives—comparing the advantages and disadvantages of sewing clothes and buying ready-made articles, questioning why poor sewing skill is shameful in women and not in men, and interviewing a priest of the Myojin-sama with idea-oriented business methods. In addition, the contemporary trend is to use an article once and discard it. In such times, maintaining a sense of gratitude to worn, old needles is pointless. For that matter, girls these days don't use needles. So there's no sense talking about gratitude to a needle.

A needle is just one example. We live in a time when concentrating on a skill and focusing our minds on one thing (for example, a needle) is difficult. Acquiring a skill is generally considered a hobby, not indispensable in life. So inevitably the zest of sewing we learn as a hobby differs from the appeal of sewing which women learned in order "not to let their husbands and children go in rags." Today, when new products are developed one after another, and an electric appliance bought only six months ago is regarded as old, using an article with care for a long time and feeling a sense of gratitude to it requires intellectual effort.

Readers may take all these changes in our contemporary world for granted, but I am obliged to enumerate these changes as if apologizing for this book, because so many qualities that form the charm of *My Asakusa* are now lost.

It is said that a *shobu* [sweet flag] bath will keep you from illness in the course of the year. "Does it really do good?" Sawamura-san in her girlhood asked her mother. "I don't know about that. But let's keep company with the world and say it does," replied her mother and rubbed her face with a *shobu* leaf. But in the middle of that night her mother's face became swollen, and she ran a high fever. The bathhouse owner's wife came to inquire after her. The mother said cheerfully, "A germ doesn't carry a name tag. Nobody knows how the germs came into my body."

This episode has a further charm I won't discuss now, but this mother is always doing what postwar teaching has regarded as bad. She is unscientific, acts without thinking to "keep company with others," stops short of clarifying where responsibility lies, and so on. If we enumerate these points, we will laugh at the great number of them. Yet why is the mother so charming, and even beautiful? In this way, although *My Asakusa* seems like a collection of innocent reminiscences, its overflowing charm has the power to make us question our way of life and our habits of daily living to their foundation.

"I won't take responsibility for what you say of my work," Sawamura-san may scold me. "Don't write anything esoteric, or it will discourage prospective readers."

She is right. This is a book you will enjoy, reading one or two of its essays each day while appreciating their lively, crisp style. This is a book you will regret finishing because it is too good. Every time I read it, I find myself gently reproved for my way of living, my character, my boorishness, and other negative qualities.

—Taichi Yamada

✦ *Author's Note* ✦

WHEN I SAW MR. YASUJI HANAMORI AT THE office of the publishers of *Kurashi-no-Techo* [Notes on Daily Living], he suggested that I write of my childhood under the title of *Watashi no Asakusa [My Asakusa]*. His proposal was so sudden I was a little confused. Indeed I was born in Asakusa and lived there until the spring of my twenty-second year. But it has been almost forty years since I left. I hardly know anything about the contemporary Asakusa. "That's no problem at all," he told me. "I want you to write, not about any other person's Asakusa, but the Asakusa that lives in you because you were born and bred there." Mr. Hanamori might have sensed Asakusa in my way of living every day, in the daily life of a woman—a *dobucho* [a woman who intrudes in other's lives for their benefit], impulsive, fast-talking, yet self-aware. This thought suddenly made me happy. My home as a Tokyoite is Asakusa. Wherever I live in Tokyo, I am an Asakusa girl. My character of a Shitamachi woman was nurtured by my experiences on the back alleys of the Asakusa of my youth.

When I was seated before the manuscript paper, trying to reel in the threads of my memory and wondering what to write about first, all at once scenes of the town of my childhood flooded my mind. However, the Asakusa imprinted in my mind is about the common daily life on the surprisingly antiquated streets. The people who appeared in the scenes were my parents and brothers—all dead—and the women in the neighborhood.

The faces and events were all dear to me, but these topics may not interest readers. Nonetheless, I have told trifling stories of a woman's personal life, for which I beg the reader's pardon.

While writing this book, I visited Asakusa frequently. I met many old acquaintances and childhood friends and had a wonderful time, forgetting the passage of time while recalling days long gone. I thank them all deeply. I have added to the stories serialized in the *Kurashi-no-Techo* magazine during the course of a year and have written some anew, and now they are to be published in book form. I am simply overjoyed.

Let it be recorded here that my sister, Eiko Yajima, helped me to verify the memories of my childhood.

—Sadako Sawamura

My Asakusa

Special Fruit

When *mikan* [Japanese tangerines] were in season, the produce vendor's wife often stopped me on my way home from school. One day she said, "We have special fruit today. Why don't you tell your mother?" *Mikan* were my favorites and she knew it. Obtaining some money from my mother, I ran back with a basket. The vendor's wife filled it to the top with *mikan*.

They were unbelievably cheap because they were bruised, every one of them, either because they had been squeezed in the corner of the box or had been packed too closely. With the tips of my fingers I softly peeled away the decayed part of the rind sticking to the segments underneath. The orange pulp tasted sweet and tart. It was good.

Both the seller and the buyer of the bruised *mikan* (too good to be discarded despite their flaws) regarded such a transaction as normal. The attitude of the vendor's wife did not suggest a superiority that might have made her say, "This is good enough for people of your means." Nor did Mother feel insulted, which might have caused her to say, "Do you think we cannot afford anything better than this? Don't you ever look down on us!" Both seemed to agree: They are good enough for a large family with many children. Their appearance is not very good, but they are perfectly edible. Both parties were quite at ease about this exchange.

At the bottom of this relationship lay a mutual sympathy among housewives who, living on back streets, knew each other's financial situation. "Decayed *mikan*" is the last thing they would say, though in truth that is what they were.

"O-Tei-chan*⁺, we have plenty of special fruit today! How fortunate! Very lucky! Tell your mother so."

A Chance Meeting at the Public Bath

 In the New Year of my sixteenth year, I did my hair in the *yuiwata shimada** style for the first time and went to the public bath with a cake of soap and a bottle of powder in a pail. Until then I had done my long hair in the *hittsume** style. The large *shimada** twist was so heavy it almost broke my neck. Besides that, the new hairdo made me self-conscious, and I walked with my eyes cast down.

My elder brother Tomokazu, who played female roles in the Kabuki theater, had not forgotten the Shitamachi custom of "a girl's first *shimada* hairdo in her sixteenth

---

⁺See "Address" in the Glossary. Unfamiliar words and phrases are marked with an asterisk and explained in the Glossary.

year." He took the trouble of selecting a pink tie-dyed band, a comb and hairpins, and insisted that I style my hair in that manner. Mother, who never used makeup, bought me the special facial powder.

The bath in the daytime of the New Year was not crowded—fewer than ten customers. I was relieved to find no one I knew. A neighbor would have made fun of my first *shimada* coiffure. The attendant at the bathhouse spoke to me. But I was too timid to speak, so I ignored her and disrobed quickly. Crouching in the corner of the draining floor, hoping to be unnoticed, I hastened to wash myself. When I took off the lid of the powder case, a fragrant aroma struck me. On the case was written the brand name Reito and a picture of a beautiful Western girl was pasted on it.

I spread a little of the powder on my palms and painted it on my face and neck, but it spread unevenly and left only mottled marks. I was accustomed to seeing my brothers put on makeup, and I had put liquid powder on my face before. But this was my first experience at powdering my face and neck in a public bath, made worse because I was squatting with one knee drawn up. I washed the powder off with soap, painted it again, repeating this powdering and washing for some time, until I was actually dizzy, and I began sweating profusely on the cold draining floor. My reflection in the mirror before me looked like a monstrous baker. I had already used half the powder in the bottle.

I was rubbing off the powder again when a soft hand touched my back. "Pardon me. Would you mind if I helped you?" Turning around, I saw a woman, probably thirty-five or thirty-six, her hair beautifully arranged in the stylish gingko-leaf coiffure. She was a stranger in the neighborhood. With a cold wet towel, she slowly cooled my neck, flushed red and hot. With practiced hands, she repeatedly applied and spread the powder and finally finished the work nicely. Then, with a towel soaked in hot water, she dabbed the powdered part liberally and gently said, "This way you can make the powder stay."

She was right. The superfluous powder washed away, and in the mirror my neck appeared faintly white. "Because the blood has gone to your head, you should do your face at home. Add some water to the powder, apply it a few times, dabbing just as I did, then use toilet water to make it stay." As she concluded, a smile appeared in her long, almond-shaped eyes, and she said, "You know, my dear, applying makeup creates a magical transformation. If you paint yourself too white, you'll fail in this magic and give yourself away. Do you see?"

In those days, to pay respect to a woman in the bath-house, the custom was to take her pails of clean hot water for rinsing. So after she had returned to the other corner, I brought her three pails of water as thanks. Glancing at her dressing-pail, I noticed that she had no powder left; she had used it on me. Later, I strutted home, the towel hanging from my hand. Having my neck powdered by an expert, I felt I had suddenly become a beauty.

Even now, every time I apply makeup, I tell myself not to fail in this magic and give myself away.

Hatsumode, *the First Visit to the Temple on New Year's Day*

 "Wake up, Tei-bo! We'll leave you if you don't," my brother shouted. I was too sleepy to get up, but Tomokazu was tugging my braid. Brushing off his hand and pulling the quilt over my head, I heard Mother say, "You don't have to wake up your sister. Maybe she is too young for the *hatsumode.*" Oh, yes, I remembered—midnight, the New Year, we would make our first visit to the temple. Earlier in the night, I had begged and begged my parents to take me to the *hatsumode.* It seemed I had fallen asleep in the *kotatsu**. I jumped out to find my father and brother all ready to leave.

A quilted kimono, a formal *haori* half coat, a fur muffler— clad in so many layers I was as round as a ball. Yet once I was outside, the freezing cold crawled up my body from my legs. My breath was white. The peals of the bell from the Senso-ji temple seemed very close, heralding the coming of the New Year.

Coming from our back street into the main street behind the temple housing Kannon*, I saw the roof looming against the dark sky. People going to visit the temple were streaming out of houses in twos and threes, and the crowd was growing. My brother said, "There goes Kan-chan of the bedclothes shop!" Starting to run, he slipped and fell and scraped the skin off his knee. He shouted, "Look, my very first fall of the year!" "You silly boy! Watch your step when you run!" Father scolded him. That was the very first scolding of the year, too.

The peals of the bell, symbolically cleansing us of our one hundred and eight evil passions, rang at long intervals and sounded heavy. How many more times would the bell be rung until the last peal?

Bright as day, the light from the many candles poured forth from the open doors of the main building, the pious people jostling each other to get to the front. Smoke from burning incense sticks filled the area. The sounds of the large bell incessantly ringing and the silver and copper coins tossed into the offertory box mixed with the sounds of the low clogs of people walking up and down the stone pavement of the Nakamise quarters. These sounds rose like hot air high into the pitch-dark sky.

In their livery coats, dashing young men from the sushi shops clasped their large hands in prayer. A woman was praying—maybe a seamstress, for she wore a thimble on her finger. Young women of the geisha quarters also prayed, their heads lowered. At the napes of their necks, the edges of their red undergarments peeped out. Their newly dressed *shimada* chignons smelled of pomade and were covered with tissue paper to protect them from dust. "May the New Year really be happy and prosperous!" The faces of the people absorbed in prayer were all flushed and gentle. Their harsh expressions—visible until the year-end—were gone. I could hardly believe it.

"Happy New Year!" "Happy New Year to you, too. Let's hope all will be for the best in the New Year." Eager Shitamachi people were already exchanging New Year's greetings while hustling and jostling in the crowd. Clinging to my father's sleeve so I wouldn't get lost, I arrived home, holding a red paper charm above my head as others had done, a charm that read, "May your luck improve and evils be warded off." The bells had ceased ringing.

"Get up and eat your *ozoni** [sweet rice cakes in soup] to celebrate the New Year. If you dawdle, you'll be late for the ceremony at school," Mother said as she woke me again. Outside the sun was bright. In the house the aroma of soup richly flavored with dried bonito stock and of scorched rice cakes gently floated through the house.

My father, who usually got up late, had already shaved and was seated before the oblong brazier, dressed in his checkered best clothes and a *haori* with the family crest. "Happy New Year!" Mother and we children, all dressed up—even my little brother Tokunosuke assumed an unaccustomed formal manner—bowed to Father with our fingers on the straw tatami floor mat.

"A Happy New Year to you, as well. Let's hope for the best this year, too." My father nodded to us with an affected air of indulgence. On the paper wrapper of Father's special round chopsticks for the New Year was written in the large characters of the Kantei style— "Master."

The Incident at the Candy Shop

 A candy shop stood on the back street in the Umamichi section near our house. The amiable owner was always seated in the shop. She was fat and fair complexioned, so the children nicknamed her "Aunt Piggy."

My elder brother Tomokazu, when he was nine or ten years old, was a good customer of this shop. Fulfilling his father's dream, he had become a child Kabuki actor. Every time he appeared on the stage of the Miyato Theater, the audience applauded his doll-like cuteness. My father, who was so pleased, gave him a special allowance as a reward. My brother always rushed to the candy shop with the money and, swelling with pride, bought his playmates candy and *menko** cards. The shopkeeper, all smiles, winked at me once when I was with him: "Your brother is free with his money. He will be a big success as an actor, I'm sure."

One day this lady, with a sour look on her face, knocked on our kitchen door. She held a five-yen note in her right hand and showed the money to my puzzled mother, who had come out of the back room. "Your boy paid me with this bill," she said. "Are you sure this is OK?"

At that time my brother was crazy about *ate-muki,* a rolled-paper lottery. In this lottery, many rows of tightly rolled pieces of paper about three centimeters long were pasted on a piece of cardboard a little larger than rice paper. A child paid two *sen** [one *sen* = .01 yen] and tore off his choice. If the paper was blank, he won a small piece of candy. The second or third prize was a toy fish or a flower made of frozen refined sugar. The first prize was a large piece of candy the shape of a bream and was the one the children coveted most. This superb prize always sat imposingly on the shelf smiling down on the children. When more than half the lots were drawn and the big bream still sat on the shelf, it meant that the first-prize lot was surely among the remainders. The dream of every child was to have plenty of money and say "All bought!" and then unfold all the remaining pieces to win the first-prize bream.

The shop owner's story was this: My brother came to the shop with many of the neighborhood children that day and shouted "All bought!" He then threw down that five-yen note before her. He took off a practically untouched lottery board from the wall, threw it before his friends, and exclaimed, "Pick what you like. The first and second prizes are in there." He behaved like the millionaire Kinokuniya Bunzaemon*. "Your boy says he was exceptionally good on the stage today and his father gave him the money as a reward. But don't you think five yen is a little too much for a child?" the woman asked. In those days a college graduate's monthly salary was forty yen, on average.

My mother turned pale. She opened the drawer of the Buddhist family altar common to most houses those days: "Five yen is missing."

"My hunch was right, then," the shopkeeper said.

"Please don't say anything to him at the shop," my mother pleaded. "I'll give him a good scolding later."

"That's the thing to do. Now here is the money," the lady replied.

"But he peeled all the lots, didn't he?" Mother said.

"Don't worry," she said. "It was wrong of me not to have stopped him at once." The woman pressed the note into my mother's palm and was about to go. But turning back, she said sheepishly, "Well, maybe I'd better take the money after all. Profit from our business is small, so let me take the original cost. I'll bring the change later." Taking the bill, she hurried away.

Soon my brother, the triumphant Kinokuniya Bunzaemon, came home. How severely my mother punished him that night! "If you take even your parents' money without permission, you are a thief. If I let this pass unpunished now, you may end up stealing from others." She spanked him hard on his small bottom ten times. She would have punished him further and more severely; however, my father, who had just come home, intervened.

"Please forgive me, Mother. I'll never do it again, I promise," my brother cried. Tomokazu, who was chicken-hearted and spoiled, cried and cried until his eyelids were red and swollen, so that the powder for the next day's stage would not stay on his face.

Father, who indulged my brother, grumbled, "Poor boy! The old hag be damned, an unwanted tale-teller!" But Mother shook her head: "We must thank our neighbors for their concern for our children. We are often too busy to notice what is going on." This was a rare occasion when I saw her contradict Father.

My brother smiled and said of our usually gentle mother, "Her furious expression that night is still etched in my memory." This was shortly before he died at the age of sixty-eight.

Gensui the Top-Spinner

The sight of a red or a green top spinning reminds me of my childhood toothaches. Because I liked taffy and used to fall asleep while chewing it, several baby teeth had decayed. When a toothache made me cry, my mother put a bitter medicine called *konjisui* on the tooth. If that did not help, she took me on her back to a man called Gensui the top-spinner, who lived in a tenement house in the back street nearby. As I understand, he sold tooth powder in the precincts of the Senso-ji temple in Asakusa, attracting customers by demonstrating his top-spinning feats. When asked, he extracted children's decayed teeth. My neighborhood had no dentist.

In his home, a slender cord was stretched taut from the low ceiling to a pillar. Gensui spun a big top, then a small one, down one after another on the cord: "Look, look! They are spinning, spinning. Look at Gensui's tops spinning." For a moment I forgot about my aching tooth and gaped admiringly at the top. In an instant my decayed tooth was extracted. Gensui's pliers were quick. Everything was already over when I burst out crying.

When I started getting my permanent teeth, my mother did the pulling for me. She tied a white cotton thread tightly around my loose tooth and left six inches of thread in my mouth. This was for me to pull from time to time and make the tooth even looser. I pulled it often while playing beanbag or marbles. "It's about time," my mother decided. Then with her left hand on my jaw and a finger of her right hand entwined with the thread's end, she pulled the thread forcefully, and the tooth came out. What remained was for me to gargle with strong salt water. The momentary pain was severe enough to make me jump, but I was afraid my mother would scold me if I did: "A girl of your age should be able to stand that much pain." I always swallowed my salty tears together with the salt water.

If it was an upper one, I threw the extracted tooth under the floor, and if it was a lower tooth, up on to the roof, with a shout, "Turn into a mighty ogre's tooth." I was told a strong tooth would come if I threw the extracted one vigorously.

But my permanent teeth are all poor ones—perhaps because I didn't throw it vigorously enough.

Sending off the Souls of the Dead

 From January 12 to 18, constant sutra chanting came from the Hall of Kannon. Many priests took turns, several at a time, in reciting sutra without interruption. This yearly event was called "Sending Off the Dead." Believers who had recently lost their relatives brought offerings for their hungry souls. They prayed "May their souls rest in peace!" clasping their hands amid the solemn waves of sutra chanting. On the night of the eighteenth, children gathered around the hall and waited for the end of the recitation. The priests then walked around the hall waving about torches to send off the souls to Paradise. This beautiful spectacle was what the children wanted to see.

As they watched this fiery procession from under the eaves of the hall, children picked up the embers that fell to the ground and ran home triumphantly to show their mothers, a custom in those days. The burned piece of wood was considered a charm, protecting its holder from evils for the remainder of the year. I recall one time when the child of the produce vendor found one of these special embers. "Look, my child picked this large piece. Let's divide it," his mother said to the wife of the fishmonger and an old woman who lived behind their shops. All had gathered at the corner for the festivities and were overjoyed with that ember.

Young Toyo-chan, a new apprentice at the hairdresser's next door, nervously took the black, burned piece in her palm and asked, "What is this good for?"

"Good for? It keeps away evils," said the vendor's wife.

"What evils?" Toyo-chan questioned.

"Well," repied the vendor's wife, quoting an old maxim, "'an earthquake, a thunderbolt, a fire, a father,' and such."

The old woman nodded in agreement and said, "Indeed earthquakes and fires are frightful! As for thunderbolts, we occasionally scold our children like thunder, so they are sort of our relatives."

Toyo-chan, who was a bit presumptuous, cast an upward glance at the women, all of whom always had opinions on everything, and asked, without the customary charm of a young girl, "Do you . . . dread your husbands, too?"

"Yes, we do," said the produce vendor's wife, who habitually had loud fights with her husband. "They say, 'A husband is the ruler of the home.' You will marry and start a home some day, won't you? Keep this ember with good care. Then the Buddha will keep your husband from 'going to another woman,' as they say, which is the greatest evil that can befall women like us." Then all the women looked at each other, laughed boisterously, and went home, each carefully holding a piece of the ember in both hands.

In those days, the wives of Shitamachi* possessed a good-humored sense of solidarity. Sharing with one another, even a charm, increased the happiness of all.

Dondonyaki

 After the war, neat and smart *okonomiyaki* shops sprang up in many places. That puzzled me. "I wonder if adults ever eat that," I recall saying. *Okonomiyaki* is what we used to call *dondonyaki* and, as I remember, was a treat eaten exclusively by children on a cold winter day. My mother would spread a thin matting in the corridor near the kitchen and there place a portable charcoal-burning clay cooking stove. Seeing this, both my elder brother Tomokazu, then in primary school, and my younger brother Tokunosuke shouted with joy, "Hurrah! *Dondonyaki!*" They called in their neighborhood friends, and they all fought to take their seats around the stove. Mother baked flour mixed with water on a small griddle placed on the stove. Then she added minced green onions and tiny shrimp. What bliss we had blowing it cool and then eating the cake! Occasionally we had a deluxe variety with sweetened *adzuki* beans wrapped in it.

Though I was little, being a girl, I did a better job in baking *dondonyaki* than the boys did. Once, just when I took a piece of *ikaten* (*dondonyaki* with squid legs mixed in) onto my small plate, Tomokazu said, "Tei-bo, go and fetch some more flour." I ran to the kitchen and returned to take my seat, when this time my little brother Tokunosuke cried, "Sister, we have no soy sauce." I rose again, got some soy sauce, and returned to find my piece of *ikaten* gone.

"How mean of you—to send me to the kitchen and eat my cake while I'm gone!" I complained and pouted.

"Stop griping. You're only a girl," said my elder brother indifferently.

"That's right. You're a sassy girl, O-Tei*," Tokunosuke had the nerve to say.

Such teasing was typical. When they had enough *dondonyaki,* the boys would soon begin to play, often noisy pretend battles. But I was expected to put away the plates and chopsticks they left in a mess and wipe clean the matting which they stained with no thought of me.

Every time we had *dondonyaki*, I used to pray earnestly to Buddha, "Let me be born a boy in my next existence."

Our Houses in Asakusa

 I have no memory of the house where I was born in Senzoku-machi, Asakusa, because, as I was told, a flood forced us to move when I was two. The earliest house I can recall was very close to that one, on a side street of Umamichi-machi, a one-storied house with two rooms: one six mats, the other four-and-a-half.

Across the lane from our house was a stone fence with long nails along the top as a protection against burglars. The gate was the back gate of a moneylender's house, but I never saw the iron door open. I remember we used to play house on the matting we spread before the gate. I knew nothing of the people living there, but I had heard they were richer than anyone in the area.

Our neighbor to the right was our landlord. He also owned a pawnbroker's shop, a secondhand clothes store, and a storehouse, so he must have been rich. The rest of the houses in the neighborhood were more or less small dwellings like ours and were built so closely together that if we ran out of our house recklessly we bumped our heads against the screens of our neighbor's house.

About the time I started school, we moved into a house in Saruwaka-machi. It was about the same size as the former one, but it had a second floor with one room. I was overjoyed and all day ran up and down the stairs with my brother until my father got annoyed and scolded us.

The theaters of the three Kabuki Saruwaka companies used to be in this area. Our house was near the warehouse for the Fujinami stage properties, still foremost in the Kabuki world. Even then the neighborhood included the dwellings of many theatrical people. The name Saruwaka-machi disappeared in the postwar period. How I miss it!

Next door on the right, a mother and her son, a clerk, lived quietly. On our left was a hairdresser's shop. Across the street from us a fat red-faced cobbler and his apprentice made shoes. His next-door neighbor was a lame man squatting cross-legged before his tailor's board, sewing kimonos. When a garment was finished, his wife, a slender, neat woman delivered it.

These were all small, cozy, two-storied houses, and on their small wooden balconies were pots of flowers— *omoto* [Rhodea Japonica] and *tokonatsu* [China pink]. The lattices and windowpanes were spotless, and the lane before the row of houses had no litter at all.

A Man's Age

 The night before Setsubun*, Mother placed soybeans on a tray and was sorting out bad ones. We children were overjoyed: "Hurrah! Tomorrow is Setsubun." February 3, traditionally the day before the first day of spring, meant bean-throwing at the Senso-ji temple, which was a bit different than the custom elsewhere.

Clothed in ceremonial *kamishimo** dress, believers, chosen from among those born under the year's zodiac sign, scattered beans. This part was typical of Setsubun festivities. At Senso-ji, in addition, the chosen scattered paper talismans from above the pillars of the main building, and both children and adults eagerly picked them up.

The moment the talismans were dropped, a priest nearby waved them away with a large fan, half the size of a *shoji** [the sliding doors used in Japanese homes]. The small talismans flew upward on this skillfully created breeze and came down like dancing flower petals. Moving to right and left like waves, the crowds in the precincts cried each time, "There! There they go." "Look! Here they come." Children nimbly ran about among the adults and picked them up quickly: "I've got two." "Look! Mine is three." They competed with one another, boasting of their achievements, their cheeks red. That was fun. The children never minded that in the excitement they sometimes scraped their foreheads or scratched their arms. Nothing so minor made the scamps or tomboys cry. Clicking his tongue, a child applied his own saliva on the wound and then forgot about it.

In the evening, we had a bean-throwing in our house too. With a grave face and carrying a one-*sho* [half-gallon] measure under his arm, my father threw beans everywhere in the small house, shouting, "In with good fortune! In with good fortune!" If we picked up and ate as many beans as equaled our age, we were supposed to be free from illness during the year. The beans carefully roasted on an earthen pan were fragrant, soft, and delicious. We counted thirteen for Tomokazu, ten for me, and seven for Tokunosuke, and munched them and some more as a treat.

My mother, who was over forty, laughed, saying she could not possibly eat that many, while my father ate only a few. "Father, how many are you supposed to eat?" I asked. "Silly! Do you dare to ask a man to tell his age?" he said, glaring at me. Pretending to scowl, he straightened himself up, took up the measure with an air, opened the latticed door, and threw beans outside. "Out with evil! Out with evil!" He looked chic, like a handsome actor.

The fact was that, being eleven years older than my mother, father was over fifty then. I knew that, but I didn't ask further, for the sake of his honor.

The Small Matter of a Husband's Flirtations

 "Flirting with women other than his wife proves that a man is somebody"—all men in the Asakusa area seemed to think so. This thinking was not limited to the men. Even the women accepted it. They did not do so willingly; they were just resigned to such behavior.

Not infrequently, a husband took advantage of this resignation and went too far. His wife would explode, and a scuffle would ensue. On such occasions some local men would jump in, separating and calming them. They would say to the man, "You have gone too far. We don't insist on complete fidelity, but why don't you be more discreet?" Then they would try to appease his wife: "Stop making a scene, my dear. It's nothing more than your husband's nature. Be patient." In most cases such words settled the fight. I know of a few cases where a couple divorced because of the husband's infidelity. The women with whom the men had affairs were mostly from the geisha quarters.

When my father married my mother, the most popular geisha of Asakusa sent him a box of dried bonito as a wedding gift. Inside, she placed a carving knife. This was one of my father's boastful stories. My father was a tall, oval-faced, handsome man in the fashion of an earlier time, and any number of geisha were ready to spend money lavishly on dates with him. When he wanted fun, he never lacked women.

The reason that he, at long last, thought of marrying at thirty-six was that he wanted to raise boys of his own as Kabuki actors. "I know a girl of the type you want, a girl who is strongly built and durable," said his acquaintance, an old clothes dealer. My mother was twenty-five when he quickly made the marriage arrangements. She was a lively, hardworking woman, but she was dark skinned, large boned, and could hardly be called a beauty.

The next day, after the shortest of wedding ceremonies was performed, a geisha called for him. She left her message with his new wife, and my father, with a nonchalant air, went to see her. This kind of behavior went on for about twenty years. Yet I never saw my parents actually quarrel or fight.

Once, when my father was upstairs merrily flirting

with a girlfriend, my mother silently made tea downstairs and had me take it to them. My young girl's heart was devastated by my father's behavior, and I asked my mother why she did not protest. "I am an unsophisticated, plain woman, so it can't be helped," she said and turned away.

Be that as it may, I wonder why my mother, a strong-minded and shrewd woman, put up with all that. My father's insensitivity certainly went beyond the limit, and he was never discreet. So my mother must have endured patiently, convinced it was unbecoming of her to show jealousy of her husband's women.

Asakusa was really the wanton man's paradise.

Needles Stuck in Tofu

 February 8 is the day for the memorial service for needles. Together Asakusa women visit the Awashima Myojin in the precincts of Senso-ji. Awashima-sama is a deity of sewing. In those days sewing was the most important skill required of Shitamachi girls. "If you are a poor seamstress, your husband and children will go in rags. It's a discredit to a woman," my mother used to say.

My mother taught me the basics of needlework, from quilting a dustcloth to sewing a kimono, a *haori* [a half coat], and a *hakama* [a formal skirt]. She was strict in teaching such fundamentals as plying a needle and wearing a thimble. "When you do the cutting, first offer a magical prayer," she said. We would measure the length of the cloth, fold it for the cutting according to the traditional practice, and take up the scissors. We put the scissors on our chest and recited, "Please, Awashima-sama, please help me not to err in the cutting." Repeating this three times calmed the mind. Then, making sure of the correct folding, we cut the cloth. As long as we did this, we were not afraid of cutting into the shoulder by mistake and embarrassing ourselves.

Awashima-sama is a kind deity and always answers our prayers, but gets angry if we treat our needles carelessly. Whenever we began to sew, we first counted the needles in the pincushion and counted them again when we finished. If even one needle was missing, we searched for it until we found it. In this way no one was likely to get hurt by a needle lying on the *tatami* mat or by one carelessly left in a neckband. "One who uses needles carelessly gets punished by Awashima-sama and remains a poor seamstress all her life," my mother used to say. So I carefully kept broken or bent needles in a small box my mother gave me and offered them to Awashima-sama at the yearly memorial service for needles.

My mother's elder sister, Aunt O-Tomi, was a perfect seamstress. Women said that even long years of wear would not stretch her kimonos out of shape, and women from the geisha quarters placed orders with her year-round. My aunt, who was too self-conscious to say anything in public, taught each of her many pupils kindly and, with her short body bent, plied her needle from early morning to late at night. She supported her nagging foster mother, an ex-geisha, solely by her sewing and had forsaken any chance for marriage. "This is my destiny and I accept it," she said and never complained. This attitude vexed my mother, a woman of spirit, who wished for her sister's happiness.

When tired from sewing, Aunt O-Tomi used to make a variety of things with waste pieces for "her little niece," such as bedclothes for my little doll or a money pouch. The gift that still lives in my memory is a miniature fruit basket, two centimeters in diameter, woven with strings made by sewing black crepe cuttings in the form of slender paper strings. When she made apples and strawberries with red and green silk fragments and piled them up in the basket, her slender fingers looked like magic wands. Watching her, I held my breath in admiration. A smile was on her face.

Once a year my aunt went out happily, with her head raised and her body straight. That was the day of the memorial service for needles. That day the hairdresser fixed my aunt's hair in the *obako* style and, wearing her best clothes—a striped double-ply kimono—my aunt, cheerful and lively, visited Awashima-sama. At those times, she was a different person. I still recall her words: "We thrust broken needles into a cake of tofu when we offer them to Awashima-sama. We want to thank and console the needles for their long and strenuous struggle with hard cloth." Saying this, she turned to me, who was by her side, and smiled.

Her face was filled with unspoken pride in being financially independent through her skill.

The Taste of Mother's Meals

 My father always ate catered meals. His favorites were *sashimi* [slices of raw fish], *tempura* [deep-fried fish and vegetables], and *unagi* [broiled eel]. On the rare occasions when he ate at home in the evening, Mother sent me to buy these special dishes. I often recall my father eating sashimi with his thick ivory chopsticks, indifferent to the fact that at the same table his wife and children were eating *satoimo** and *konnyaku**, inexpensive vegetables, seasoned with soy. None of the family thought this strange or objectionable.

My mother, therefore, did not have to cook to please my father's palate. Her daily task was to prepare tasty meals to feed her growing children within the small budget my father provided, so she was always busy in the kitchen. Frequently, she simmered chopped potatoes and carrots and minced beef in a deep pot, to which she added flour for thickening and salt for seasoning. After cooking the mixture for a long time, this was her stew. If she added curry powder to the stew and spread it on hot rice, she called it curried rice. Glancing at this, my father said with a frown, "Looks like a Western dish in a back-country restaurant." Yet my brothers and I all liked it and asked for more, each wanting to be served first.

Behind our house was a shop that sold river fish, and when it had a bargain on *mezokko* [small eels], we had a feast—bowls of broiled eels and rice. Mother fanned a fire made in the clay charcoal stove, and a delicious aroma spread through the house. If my mother's purse were nearly empty, she bought *okara,* the leftovers from making tofu, and fried it, adding her special sauce. "Look," she said, "We have fried pork cutlet minus the pork." We didn't think that was unusual at all—such poor and sometimes unpalatable fare tasted good because Mother was there, sitting beside us looking at us eagerly, all smiles.

Mother's pot boiled and simmered in the kitchen all year round. She prepared *ami* [small shrimp-like crustaceans], which was sold by the *sho,* about a half-gallon, in soy to preserve them. Another of her favorites was boiled-down kelp and soybeans seasoned together. Every year when winter came, Mother boiled and sweetened *adzuki* beans as the base for *oshiruko* soup. After the New Year's celebration, she cut the *kagami mochi,* the round rice cakes offered to the gods, into small pieces which she dried and fried to the core so that they became crisp and fragrant. Then she put these special snacks in a can in the tea cabinet.

We children used to regard our mother, who created these delights, as a perfect cook. However, when I am asked what dish my mother prepared best, I am at a loss for an answer. She was driven by household chores every day and racked her brains to prepare meals with inexpensive ingredients. She did not seem to have any particular dish that was her speciality. When she served nutritious and tasty dishes to her children, however, every plate brimmed with her love and motherly thoughtfulness.

Young people today say they yearn for the "taste of their mothers' cooking." But isn't their real craving for the "seasoning of love"?

Meeting Hei-san at the Miso* *Shop*

 I was born sensitive to both heat and cold. In summer, I was always hot and suffered severely, yet in winter my arms and legs were always chilled, and I constantly had a cold. My mother said that my pale lips and frequent dizzy spells were the result of the whooping cough I had soon after I was born. In those days, nobody had heard of low blood pressure, the real cause of my ailments.

When I was covered with goose bumps because of the cold, even when wearing a quilted kimono and a heavy *haori**, my mother spread thick patches of unprocessed silk filaments on my back. A few of these silk pads inserted between my undershirt and kimono warmed my whole back from the shoulders to the waist. The same material rolled into a collar protected my throat and eased my coughing. Some of the neighborhood boys made fun of me, saying, "She looks like a puppy wearing a collar." Even with these precautions, I always had a chronic cold.

When women's woolen underwear went on sale, my mother immediately bought me a pink woolen undershirt. I was grateful for her consideration. But I had just started attending high school and had quickly grown taller, and my breasts had begun to develop. So I was never happy wearing the *miyako* underskirt—a thick, tube of rough, red wool that made the wearer look shapeless. When my mother said, "Look. Here's a new *miyako* that looks very warm," I was miserable. But she insisted: "You are sensitive to the cold, so the *miyako* is just what you need. Try it on at once." I reluctantly did so and had to wear it throughout the cold weather.

In those days, one of my tasks was to buy *miso* [a salty, soy paste flavoring] a few times each month at a large shop called the Mankyu near the Asakusa Primary School. In the shop were rows of *miso* tubs and many young men busily working. Seeing me enter the shop, some young man was sure to shout, "Hey, Hei-san, here she comes." Looking embarrassed, Hei-san, a well-built young man with a square jaw, piled *ama-miso,* the less salty kind, and regular *miso* on a bamboo husk. He ignored the rising arm of the scale and always gave me a generous portion, even an extra scoop free. "You are just the one to go buy *miso,*" mother used to say in good humor. I then assumed a prim indifference, but inwardly I was a little flattered.

One cold afternoon in February when it looked like light snow would fall any minute, Mother suddenly decided she needed some *miso* and sent me to buy it. Dressed in my usual winter clothing and with a thick woolen shawl around my neck, I soon stood in front of the Mankyu. Chill crawled up my legs from the cold earth floor and made me shiver. As usual, the young men teased me when Hei-san gave me the package of *miso* wrapped in a bamboo sheath. I was about to give him the money which I held firmly in my hand, numb from the cold, when Hei-san whispered into my ear: "Why don't you go to the movies on the first of next month with me? I can take a day off then." I was so taken aback my breath almost stopped. My face flushed.

I almost threw the money on the counter. I turned around and was about to run. But fate was cruel. The new wooden soles of my clogs slipped on the frozen earth floor. I fell flat on my face. One of the young men shrieked wildly, "Look. A red slip." "Ah, a *miyako*," another shrieked wildly. Hurriedly, I rose to my feet as they giggled behind my back.

I barely suppressed my impulse to cry and rushed home. Without a word, I handed the *miso* to my mother in the kitchen. In the corner of the back room, I took off the *miyako*, wrapped it in a cloth wrapper, and put it deep in the closet. I was overcome with shame. I was angry at everybody. After that incident, nothing my mother said could persuade me to buy the *miso* again. The red *miyako* remained in the closet and was destroyed in the fire of the Great Kanto Earthquake later that year.

That was in the winter of my fifteenth year, when I was entering adolescence.

The Riddle

 "Question: What is *wasabi* [Japanese horse-radish] like?
Answer: *Wasabi* is like a lazy girl.
Question: Why?

Answer: She lets the *wa* [the bronze hoop on a rice tub] get *sabi* [tarnished]."

With stern looks on their faces, mothers would have their daughters recite this riddle when they did not clean wooden rice tubs carefully enough.

Back in the days before electric or gas rice cookers, rice was boiled in an iron pot. When cooked, the rice was transferred to a wooden tub and then was carried into the dining area. Young girls had the task of keeping the bronze hoops on the rice tub shining bright. Every day, they had to scrub it forcefully with a scrub brush and polishing powder. Otherwise a dark green patina soon appeared, and their mothers would scowl at them.

Not only were rice tubs meticulously cleaned, but also pots and kettles, the sink, the corridors, the ceilings, the latticed door of the entrance—they were also thoroughly scrubbed and polished in the homes of Shitamachi. The wood frames of latticed doors were often worn thin because of frequent scrubbing.

Mothers often spoke this reprimand: "It is a woman's work to keep the house tidy above all so that her husband and children can be comfortable there. A draggletail is the last thing I want you to be." The "draggletail" they had in mind was a girl who wore her kimono trailing its bottom, who became engrossed in applying makeup in broad daylight, and who spent her daytime hours idly lying about: "Such a woman wears an undershirt with a dirty collar and has dirt behind her ears." Mothers unsparingly trained their daughters to keep a clean house, and daughters endured the strict training with grace.

Both mothers and daughters were convinced that the greatest insult for a Shitamachi girl was to be called a "draggletail."

My Hina Matsuri Dolls

 It seems to me that, when I was a child, I had no dolls to display for Hina Matsuri, the Doll's Festival*, which occurs annually on March 3. You may wonder why I say "It seems." The reason is that, while I have at least one or two memories of our celebrations, I have no memory at all about the dolls themselves.

I recall that every year I helped Mother take out the wooden tiers, set them up in the alcove of the upstairs room, and cover them with a red carpet. I distinctly remember the red of the carpet. However, swords, dolls of armored warriors, Kintaro* [a legendary boy of great strength] and Shoki-sama* [a Chinese ogre who repels illness] were displayed on the tiers. So my memories are of the dolls of Tango no Sekku*, that is, of the Boys' Festival, which we celebrated for my brothers every May 5. I suppose that for my father, who would go any length to celebrate Tango no Sekku, Hina Matsuri for girls was not of much concern.

One particular Hina Matsuri does stand out in my memory. In my first year of school, my mother invited a few of my friends the evening before the festival. She had spread a piece of red flannel on the living room floor and on it displayed paper dolls which my Aunt O-Tomi, the master seamstress, had made—dolls of ladies-in-waiting, townsfolks' daughters, women of mature age, children, and young Kabuki actors. In front of the multicolored paper dolls, we ate *adzuki* rice with a hot bowl of white miso soup, as well as sweetened puffed rice which we ate with our fingers. My little friends cried with joy to see the beautiful dolls; it was a proud moment for me. So, because of my aunt's beautifully made paper imitations, I had no particular wish for a traditional pair of graceful Emperor and Empress dolls.

Shortly before graduation from high school, I went to Nara on a school excursion. At an old doll shop, I found a pair of rough-hewn Emperor and Empress dolls. I thought they were beautiful. So I spent what little money I had to buy them. It was an expensive purchase for me and may indicate that in the back of my child's mind I had yearned for such dolls. For four or five years after that, at every Hina Matsuri Festival, I placed these Emperor and Empress dolls on a little table by the entrance of our home and celebrated the occasion by myself. After that, I had many changes in my life and forgot all about those dolls.

After the long Pacific War finally ended, I discovered, among the articles my mother had stored in a place safe from the bombings, a cracked box containing my dolls. I was as happy as a little girl. The Emperor and Empress looked a little timeworn but were still seated as beautifully as before.

Now I keep the pair on a living-room shelf, not only on March 3 but throughout the year. This is to make up for neglecting them for so long.

The Show Window

 When I was a young girl, a shop near the Miyato Theater installed a glass display window, the first of its kind in the area. The shop, primarily devoted to selling neckpieces, was a major subject of conversation. A tatami mat, three by two feet, sat in the window. Three terraced shelves displayed, in addition to fancy neckpieces, small articles, such as *obi-age* and *obi-dome* [accessories for the *obi*, or kimono sash]. In the corner stood a smiling Kyoto doll. Before this window was installed, we were unable to see these articles unless we entered the shop. Afterwards, to the great delight of the girls, we could see them whenever we passed the shop. At that time, few people had even heard the phrase "show window."

Curious to know the latest fashions, I often walked past the shop on my way home from *nagauta** singing practice or sewing lessons. "What a beautiful color!" I thought, seeing a neckpiece that I particularly liked. Without thinking, I leaned forward and before I knew it, the forelock of my *momoware** [the hairstyle worn by city girls in their midteens] touched the glass. When I finally stopped staring, the polished glass had stains from my hair oil and face powder. This happened often.

Once when I had dirtied the window, I got flustered and began to clean the glass with the tip of my sleeve. The shop owner saw me and called from the counter, "Look at yourself, young lady. Your hair is a mess and your powder has come off. Unless you fix your makeup and straighten your hair, your mother will know you didn't come right home. Don't worry about the glass. Straighten up!" This wonderful, plump man never scolded any of the girls who window-shopped. If this had not been Asakusa, the shopkeeper would have made some rude remark to a girl like me, who looked but never bought and just stained his window. He probably would have posted a sign saying, "DO NOT TOUCH! Please stay at least three steps from the window."

The shops of Asakusa were a customer's paradise; the shopkeepers cared more about people than about appearances.

The Festival of "The First Horse Day" at Hikan Inari Shrine

 Asakusa's Hikan Inari Shrine held its Hatsu-uma, the Festival of "The First Horse Day,"+ in March. Other Inari shrines erected on a landlord's grounds in the neighborhood or in theaters celebrated the festival on the First Horse Day in

---

+See *"junishi"* in the Glossary. Using the ancient Chinese system of astrology (similar to the Western zodiac signs), the Japanese days bear the names of twelve animals, which are repeated in sequence. Hence, a given month will have more than one "Horse Day," the seventh animal of the twelve.

Hikan means minor or subordinate; Inari, a Shinto deity of the harvest.

February according to the common custom. But the Hikan Inari Shrine (erected behind Asakusa Shrine, which in turn is beside the Senso-ji temple) celebrated its Hatsu-uma Festival on March 18 every year, a long-established practice.

On this very day, more than a thousand years ago [628 A.D.], so the legend goes, a fisherman salvaged the principal image of the Senso-ji temple—an approximately two-inch, pure gold image of the Kannon Buddha from Asakusa's Uramiyato River. The Hikan Inari Shrine's Hatsu-uma Festival may commemorate this day. If the day were established to demonstrate Hikan Inari's gratitude to Kannon for letting him use part of the precincts, this suggests that, in Asakusa, gods and buddhas alike never forget favors they receive. The elders say this shrine was donated by Shinmon Tatsugoro, well known for his chivalrous spirit. So the significance of this date is understandable.

At any rate this day was unreservedly a children's festival, and parents freed them from all chores, such as running errands to the vegetable shop or caring for babies. Children hardly arrived home from school when they threw down their schoolbags at the entrance and flew to the Hikan Inari Shrine from which the drumbeats had been sounding since morning. Parents not only did not scold them for this behavior, but even ran after them to give them spending money, saying, "Don't overeat and get an upset stomach."

Around the Inari shrine, *jiguchi-andon,* lanterns with clever wordplay written on them, hung on a rope—proud donations from each block of the town. All enjoyed comparing the puns that competed with one another for their excellence. The stone pavement leading to the *torii**, the shrine archway, was lined on both sides with small booths that sold figures shaped from *ame* [a soft malleable candy] or rice flour, cotton candy, balloons, and sweetened beans (recognizable by the hawker's familiar cry, "Hey, sweet beans for you, Kin-chan!"). A lean candy man blew into a slender bamboo pipe, like a glassblower, and inflated a soft white lump *ame* at its tip, cleverly twisting and shaping it with his fingers and painting it with red and blue pigment, quickly producing a pigeon or a rabbit.

A bald, fat craftsman who shaped rice flour, *oshinko*, had a table as cleanly polished as a chopping board. On it, he displayed imitation bowls of chowder and variously colored food made of rice flour, with plenty of syrup poured on them. The sight made our mouths water.

When the children had had enough fun eating, the boys competed with each other in drum beating, and the girls performed various tricks with beanbags, laughing merrily at the shrine until it was quite dark.

The Spring Equinox

 Until I was about age eight or nine, my family's annual visit to our ancestral gravesite was a source of especially great pleasure for me. I was told that the temple my family belonged to had formerly been located in Asakusa. But shortly before I was born, the streets were widened and lots readjusted, so the temple was relocated to Higashi-Nakano, in the suburbs of Tokyo. To Shitamachi people back then, Higashi-Nakano was the distant countryside.

Every year at the spring equinox, Father took Tomokazu and me to visit our family gravesite. From the train windows, the fields of rape flowers spread like gold carpets. Walking from the station, we followed a path between rice fields to the temple where lovely violets and dandelions peeped forth here and there.

To me, who had grown up in Asakusa where houses stood in rows, their eaves almost touching, this country scene was as beautiful as the backdrop for an elopement scene in a play. On the way, my brother proudly taught me about local vegetation, pointing to the "grass that bore rice grains" and "a tree that produced *kon'nyaku**" [a gelatinous vegetable substance]. My short-tempered father was less impressed by the beauty. Once when I wandered to another path to collect some *renge,* Chinese flowers, for a bouquet, he severely scolded me.

Our visits to the ancestral grave were short and simple. We offered flowers and lit incense sticks, poured some water from a pail on the gravestone, and clasped our hands lightly in prayer—that was all. Delivering a Buddhist service was not apppealing to my father at all. Whenever possible, he avoided long sutra chanting even when honoring his parents. On such occasions, when the fat, gentle priest clad in a gold brocade vestment solemnly seated himself before the figure of Amitabha, a Buddhist deity, and took up his thick sutra book,

Father would call to him from behind, "Please, sir, make it short; just read the most important part. I have some business I must attend to." With his back to us, the priest nodded slightly, and his sutra chanting ended soon after. The priest showed no sign of displeasure toward my father, an irreverent believer. No doubt Father's donation was also small.

However, Father, and even Tomokazu and I, looked forward to one part of the ritual visit to the family gravesite—the "dinner eaten after purification." We always ate at Hirae-ken, a small Western restaurant. My father was a gourmet but never ate out other than in Asakusa. He used to say, "The restaurants in Asakusa are the most comfortable of any. The best part is that they aren't pretentious. Besides, the food is inexpensive and plentiful." Still Hirae-ken was special. It had only three tables and could seat only ten guests at a time. My father would order fried oysters for himself and fried pork cutlets for us children. When in an especially good humor, he ordered a soup dish called *soppu* for us.

In my family, only my father, and sometimes my elder brother, ate catered dishes. They would eat first and choose the best selections. Later, my mother and I ate what they left. Only on this annual gravesite visit was I treated as an equal. Set before me was a full portion, a large piece of fried pork cutlet with plenty of chopped cabbage. I firmly believed that nowhere in the world was there a more delicious Western dish than that.

As I finished and wiped my mouth with the napkin spread beneath my chin, I always wished for the next equinox to come soon.

Street Vendors

 From early morning until dark, various vendors hawked their goods from alley to alley in Asakusa. A clog mender lowered his load to the ground beneath the eaves, then with his right hand flailed the drum in his left with a slender bamboo branch to announce his arrival. As he walked, he almost stuck his head into the houses and shouted, "Clog mending! Anyone need clogs mended?" A vendor of medicine, in those days called a *josaiya,* carried a pole on his shoulder with tall boxes on both ends and many small drawers in each. He walked slowly, keeping time with the movements of his load hanging in front of and behind him. Every time he took a step, the brass handles of the drawers rattled, producing lively sounds. Housewives stepped out, saying, "Here comes the medicine peddler." A *tofu* vendor blew his horn. And a *natto* [fermented soybeans] vendor hawked his wares in a hoarse voice: *"Natto . . . natto . . ."*

A *fukimameya,* a vendor of large, sweetened beans—perhaps he took a vacation during the midwinter—never failed to come round when it got warmer. He was an old man, as bald as an egg, and cried out in a thin, almost transparent and high-pitched voice, *"Fukima-meya . . . fukimaa . . ."* The tub he carried was washed clean, and the hoops were polished brightly.

"That *fukimameya's* wife must surely adore him. Look at those pants and his coat. They're like a quilt. If she were not so deeply in love, she wouldn't have gone to so much trouble to mend them so neatly."

"Maybe they eloped. That's my guess. His head's an egg now, but he must have been a handsome man when young. His nose is still straight."

"I'll bet you envy his wife. Me, too!"

The women were boisterous in their comments. They said they always bought his sweetened beans because they tasted good and were cheap. But I suspect the real reason was that the women liked that old man's cheerful face.

In their hearts these women adored a happy couple, but they particularly cherished an affectionate husband.

Gen-san the Fortune Teller

When I was a child, a fat fortune teller, Gen-san, who we called "Gen-san the Pock-Marked" often dropped by our house. Wearing a somewhat grimy, striped kimono and with his back slightly hunched, he always carried a package wrapped in a piece of cotton. The bundle contained divining sticks and blocks, a big magnifying glass, and a few thin books with pages of complex Chinese characters. These were the tools of Gen-san's trade.

My parents both seemed to like the cheerful Gen-san. Every time he dropped in, they treated him to a cup of *saké,* his favorite drink, and enjoyed chatting with him. However, my parents did not trust his predictions.

They even told him so: "All prophesies are chance. They may or may not come true." Gen-san himself said nothing and just grinned. Perhaps he thought so too.

One autumn day when I had just entered primary school, Gen-san was talking to me and told me something that shocked me. He said, with pride in his voice, "It was I who named you, O-Tei-chan* [see "Address" in Glossary]." I had known that my father was not pleased when I was born. He had said, "It's a girl. What a shame!" He had not bothered to name me even seven days after my birth. He had been determined to raise all his children to be Kabuki actors. So he was openly disappointed at the birth of a girl.

My mother, who could not write, was at a loss and asked Gen-san, who happened to drop in, for help in choosing a name and expressing it in appropriate characters.+ "With pleasure!" the fortune teller said and pounded his chest. Then, he slowly shuffled and squeezed his divining sticks and moved or removed divining blocks. After meditating for some time, he wrote three girls' names on three slips of paper. He placed the papers with the names face down on the *tatami* mat, shuffled them about with his eyes closed, and finally chose one. On that slip was written "Teiko."

I was not at all pleased with his story. "That's not true," I protested. "My parents chose my name after

---

+A Japanese person's family name and often the given name is written in Chinese characters, *kanji,* of which many have more than one meaning and pronunciation. For example, the Chinese character for the first part of Sawamura's given name [偵] means both "chastity" and "loyalty to a feudal lord" and is pronounced either as "sada" or "tei." (*"Ko"* [子] indicates the person is female.)

they consulted with each other." I noticed that Father pretended not to hear me. And Mother only smiled and said nothing. So I thought Gen-san's story might be true. As I recall, my brothers, who became child actors as my father wished, used to make fun of me and irritated me by saying, "Good girl, good girl, good-for-nothing girl!"

When he noticed how disheartened I was, Gen-san tried to comfort me: "Well, well, let me, your name-giver, now tell you your fortune." As if to humor me, he examined my small palm with his big magnifying glass. "Oh, my! What splendid palm lines!" he bellowed. On both my palms, from the base of the middle finger to the wrist, ran straight unbroken lines. "This is promising," he said. "You will surely be a great success. But, wait a minute, unfortunately, you're a girl. If you were a boy, you would most certainly be a general or a minister in the government. What a shame!" He sighed excessively, holding my hand. As a child, I accepted what he said and agreed. I regretted that I was not born a boy.

Soon after that my name-giver died. Mother said, "It was apoplexy, I hear. Since his wife left him, he was always drunk. But he was a very likable man. I wonder if he could tell his own fortune? I wonder if he knew."

Even now, when I look at my palms, my memory of Gen-san recurs. "Prophesies are capricious. They may or may not come true"—I feel I can hear him saying that somewhere.

I Am an Asakusa Girl!

 One day some unexpected business arose that required Mother to go to Honjo, on the other side of the Sumida River. Because she was unaccustomed to going out alone, she asked me to go with her. I was on my spring break from school. I wore my dress outfit for the trip, a blue silk kimono, the only one I owned, and a red woolen sash, an *obi.* My hair was fluffed up and held in place with an attractive comb. As we left, I felt wonderful.

Mother's business was over about noon. Though it was a little too early for the season, Mother suggested that we treat ourselves to viewing the cherry blossoms. After all, it was not often that we, mother and daughter, went on an outing together. On our way, we stopped at Mukojima, an area on the riverbank where the cherry trees were particularly attractive. While Mother went to a shop near the Chomei-ji temple to buy *sakura-mochi,* rice cakes filled with sweet bean paste then wrapped in cherry leaves, I waited alone on the riverbank. A few early cherry buds had turned red and begun to blossom, and I was gazing absentmindedly at the Sumida River.

Suddenly a thick voice from behind me said, "Hey, Honey! Hey, you over there!"

Glancing backward, I was startled at what I saw. At the foot of a cherry tree thirty or forty feet behind me seven or eight road-crewmen were sitting, eating their lunches and grinning. They were all looking my way.

"I like your red sash, little lady," one said.

Then I heard, "Waiting for somebody?"

"Let me guess. Is it your lover?"

"If he isn't here now, he isn't going to show, honey."

"How about having a little fun with me instead."

Blood rushed to my head, and my heart began pounding. I felt too weak in the knees to move. So I looked the other way and said nothing. But this only seemed to encourage them. Then one said something vulgar that made me want to cover my ears.

Another stood up and and said in a particularly high-pitched voice, mimicking a girl, "You guys are embarrassing me." They roared with laughter.

Just then, without thinking, I looked up, turned, and walked staight toward them. The laughing stopped dead. Their faces went blank, gaping at the girl who suddenly stood before them. "That is enough! This is a public street, isn't it? Can't a girl even walk down the street? What's so funny about me looking at the cherry blossoms and the river? Who I am waiting for is none of your business. Leave me alone. If you want to eat your lunch, do it. But keep your mouth shut when you look at me! Just shut up! You have no manners! You just want to make up for your miserable lunch by making fun of a girl. You're all mean. You should all be ashamed of yourselves!"

By the time I finished talking, I was delirious. My knees were shaking with anger. I felt a tugging on my left sleeve and thought it was going to come off: Mother, her face white with fear, was standing behind me and pulling me back. The men were agape and just stared at us, speechless, chopsticks in their hands. Soft sunlight poured over the cherry buds. All was silent. The wind coming over the water felt pleasantly soothing to my burning cheeks.

The silence seemed to last much longer than the five or ten seconds that actually elapsed. As I began to calm down, I was overwhelmed with shame. Then I was frightened. I felt the strength sap from my shoulders.

I nodded my head in a bow before the men and said, "I am sorry. I said too much." The group sighed in relief. Then a well-built man who seemed to be in charge stepped forward. He returned my bow with a pleasant expression and said, "We are sorry, too, Miss. I apologize." Relieved, my mother bowed slightly and pulled me quickly by the hand. We left the scene quickly.

When we were down the bank and out of the men's sight, Mother stopped, turned to me, and stared at my face, bewildered: "O-Tei, you, are usually not much of a talker, you . . ." She said how thankful she was that it ended with no harm, repeating herself many times.

That night in bed, I thought and thought: "Why did I speak with such vehemence?" I could find no answer. But I did discover one thing: I learned that after all I was a simple but determined Asakusa girl.

This was a memory of my seventeenth spring.

My First Day
at Asakusa Primary School

 I was born in November, so by the way age used to be counted I was considered a two-year-old when I was actually less than two months old. Because I was *osoumare*[+], I was enrolled in primary school at the age of eight according to *kazoe,* that is, when I was six years and six months old by the present way of counting. In those days, only children from wealthy families—landowners, doctors, moneylenders, pawnbrokers—or coddled heirs attended kindergarten. In my family, only my elder brother was allowed to attend the Tokufu Kindergarten of the Denpo-in temple in Asakusa. I envied him and impatiently awaited the day when I would start school.

I enrolled at Asakusa Primary School on April 1, in the fourth year of Taisho [1915], more than sixty years ago. This school has a long history and celebrated its one hundredth anniversary in 1973. On my first day of school, with my hair bobbed, clad in a printed woolen kimono and wearing a maroon *hakama,* a pleated over-skirt, I walked through the school gate alone. In those days, parents did not accompany their children to the entrance ceremony.

"Asakusa Primary School is a good school! But for the

[+]By the old way of counting age, *kazoe,* a child was one year old from the time of his birth until the end of the year and gained a year on every New Year's Day. A child who is *osoumare,* literally meaning "late born," is born later than April 1, the first day of the school year. Japanese children begin attending primary school the first April after they are fully six years old.

kids who attend, it's a bad school," my brother and his pals had fun chanting. However, it was the school I had dreamed about. The gym, floored with brick, looked beautiful and modern, like one in a Western country. I was nervous and tense.

Soon Ms. Kenmochi, our homeroom teacher, introduced a male teacher who was in charge of the boys. "Well, students, this is Mr. Okunuki. He and I will work together, like good friends, and help you with your studies. I hope you have understood what I have said. Raise your hand and say 'yes,' if you have."

I was listening intently in a row near the front and raised my hand enthusiastically. I was so enthusiastic I said, "Yes, ma'am, I understood. I see you two are *oka-bore,* a happy couple." The two were nonplussed and stood silently staring at me. After a time, Ms. Kenmochi looked me sternly in the face and said slowly, "It is bad manners to say something like that, child."

Realizing I had said something improper, I blushed and drooped my head. Why was it inappropriate to say *okabore*? *Okabore* meant a man and a woman getting along well, like good friends.[+] A novice geisha girl had taught me so at a *nagauta* lesson a few days before. I was in a quandary. I didn't know what to do. The teachers might say, "Don't you come to school anymore."

After all these years, I still recall Ms. Kenmochi's low pompadour and maroon *hakama* and Mr. Okunuki's black-rimmed spectacles and gray suit. I even recall the sunlight teeming down on the schoolyard. The vividness of this recollection reveals how stunned I was.

[+]The term literally means an inappropriate yearning, here, for example, one teacher coveting the other who is committed or married to another.

Asakusa's Miso * *Soup*

 In the alleys of Asakusa, every morning began with the aroma of *miso* soup. From open kitchen doors facing the narrow alleys, with house eaves almost overlapping one another, the sounds of pickles being chopped, rice bowls being set on the table, and the cries of mothers waking their sleepy children could be heard. Floating among these sounds was the smell of scorched rice. And embracing it all was the subtle aroma of *miso* soup.

The fragrant odor made me think: Our next-door neighbor may have put tofu in the soup; and the one across from us, *wakame* seaweed, or radish. My favorite *miso* soup contained *okara* [the tasty leftovers from making tofu], fried tofu, and chopped green onions. My family called this "Full House Soup" because of the "crowd" of ingredients. My father, who worked at a theater, may have supplied the name.

Shitamachi housewives mixed varying amounts of slightly salted and strongly salted *miso,* crushed it in a mortar, and strained it, further enriching the stock by adding small fish. Families all believed that their *miso* soup was the best. Asakusans started every day with as many as two or three bowls of this delicious soup.

My Burgeoning Curiosity

Soon after I started school, I was made an attendant for my little brother, who was a child actor for the Miyato Theater. From the wings, I saw Kabuki plays almost every day and, child as I was, began to ask myself, "What is a lord?"

In *Sendaihagi,* Nurse Masaoka lets her own dear child die, and the nurse in *Shigenoi Parting with Her Child* abandons her child—both acts done for the sake of feudal lords. The women in the plays are tenderhearted mothers, and the females in the audience shed tears of grief over the sad stories. The loss of the children was incomprehensible to my childish mind. I wondered, "Why did they have to make such a sacrifice for their lord?" I asked my father. He simply said, "Silly! That was the way it was in the old times; everybody accepted it." My mother didn't treat my question seriously, just saying "I am not educated, so I don't know."

From these early questions, my curiosity gradually grew strong. I wanted to learn why. I wanted to know how. I harbored a desire to study further, to continue my schooling. In the beginning, my father was displeased with the idea of his daughter going to a high school, but, giving in to my persistent requests, he finally gave his permission. But he warned me that he could not afford to pay for my further education. At that time, my older brother played female roles at the Teigeki Theater, and the formal announcement of his promotion to major actor was approaching. My family needed a significant amount of money for this occasion, and the preparation left them in a state of confusion.

Finally, my mother said she could scrape together the necessary money for me until I found a part-time job. That was how I was able to apply to a girls' high school. In March of the following year, I passed the entrance exam for the school of my choice. When I saw my name posted among the successful applicants, I flew home to tell the news, traveling the distance in far less than the hour it usually took. Our house was locked, and everybody had gone to the Miyato Theater. So I rushed off again. I found Mother preparing my younger brother in the dressing room. Hearing my news, she sighed deeply and said, "This is going to be tough." Despite her fears, I was overjoyed.

Neither of my parents ever came to my high school even once during my long years of attendance. I don't think they even knew where it was. No one in my family asked to see my report card at the end of the term; my school record was of little importance to them. Therefore, only my own desire determined the extent to which I studied. I was a bit lonely, but in my own way I found attending school and studying to be a splendid life.

Soon after beginning high school, I found a position as a tutor for the daughter of the owner of a china shop in the Nakamise quarters. Even in Asakusa in those days, the number of parents who were keen on their children's education was increasing. So I was busy every day tutoring—I, a girl still in braids.

Shiro-chan, the Baker's Daughter

 Buddha's birthday is celebrated in April. As soon as I came home from primary school that day, my little brother, Tokunosuke, who was three years younger than I, began badgering me to take him to the Senso-ji temple. When we arrived, a large crowd of children had gathered in front of the main temple where a statue of the newborn Buddha stood in a small shrine decorated with flowers. Like a sweet chorus, the priests filled the temple, softly chanting sutra in harmony.

With dippers in their hands, children struggled with one another to pour the "tea of heaven" over the Buddha's head. It was considered a prayer for the soul of Buddha if we poured "tea" (made from boiled licorice) on the statue, and in so doing we acquired virtues of the Buddha. Some children struggled to reach the head, standing on tiptoes to do so. Others stretched out their little hands, while held in their mothers' arms. A mother shouted excitedly, "No, no, a little higher. Pour it over the Buddha's head." A little boy shrieked, "Watch out! You got my kimono wet." If we picked up and treasured a petal from one of the lotus flowers the priests scattered, we believed the petal would make us happy. Asakusa had many legends of this sort.

Tokunosuke, who was at a rambunctious age, was running around and waving a dipper, singing "*Kappore! Kappore!* Drink tea of heaven and dance the *kappore* [a comical dance, inappropriate for this festival]." Just as I was giving him a good spanking, someone lightly grabbed my hand. I turned to see Shiro-chan, the baker's daughter, her round, freckled face grinning. She told me to relax and let Tokunosuke enjoy himself. She was five or six years older than I, so she must have been fifteen or sixteen. She was always cheerful and sweet, and I liked her very much. My mother always used to praise her for the way she behaved in her father's shop: "She is a really good girl. Most of all, she responds to customers very well, always pleasant. You might say she is 'beautiful when replying.'" Even when viewed in the most favorable light, one would never call Shiro-chan beautiful. She was short and stockily built, but Mother said her prompt, clear, and cheerful responses—"Yes, ma'am. Yes, sir,"—made everyone happy.

If her customer were a little boy with a runny nose, and he wanted an *anpan,* a bun filled with sweetened bean jam, she would say, "Here you are, little boy. Thank you very much. Wait a moment." And she wiped his nose for him. She was so sweet. The produce vendor's wife used to say, "It's interesting that Shiro-chan, who works so energetically and speaks so cheerfully, seems far more attractive than a girl who boasts of her beauty and wastes her time."

✦ ✦ ✦

When we met at the festival, Shiro-chan told us she was on her way home after collecting the proceeds from a sale on her father's buns at a movie house in Rokku. We pestered her to join us. She hesitated and said, "No! I can't stay." Nevertheless, we spent nearly an hour visiting one stall after another.

In the early afternoon the next day, Mother said,

"O-Tei, you were with Shiro-chan yesterday, weren't you? I heard that she lost some money, as much as four yen." I was so surprised, it almost took my breath away. Four yen was an enormous sum. The price of an *anpan* was only two *sen*, one fiftieth of a yen. I wondered when she lost the money, or whether her pocket was picked. I worried that perhaps I should not have detained her.

Her father must have severely reprimanded her. This thought almost made me cry. My mother confirmed my fears: "I hear her father got very angry and shouted at her and told her to get out of the house! He said that to his only daughter. The poor girl! When I heard him shouting, I begged him to forgive her."

Then Mother added, as if an afterthought, "Oh, that reminds me, for a while, we will be eating buns often." Because her children were partly responsible for the baker's loss, my mother decided that she would buy ten or twenty sen worth of bread at his shop every day, small help as it was. She knew the loss of four yen was a great blow to the baker, who eked out a paltry living with his apprentice. Though sorry for Shiro-chan, I was secretly disappointed to hear my mother's plan. Children in those days were not used to eating buns often. An occasional *anpan* was a novelty and tasted good, but I thought that eating them every day would make me sick.

But Mother was true to her word. Starting the next day, our daily lunch consisted of buns—every day. We had buns with bean jam, buns with other kinds of jam, and buns with cream inside. We had buns of all different shapes. In ten days, I almost retched just at the smell of them. It was worse for my father and elder brother who never liked buns. My little brother even had the nerve to say, "I hear that eating nothing but bread makes your eyes turn blue." And he refused to touch them from the third day on. Soon only Mother and I were eating them, cramming them into our mouths and forcing ourselves to chew them.

After about twenty days passed, Mother said, "I have prepared sushi for lunch today—a treat." We cheered for joy. She told us that the baker had come by the night before and said, "Shiro* [see Glossary, "Address"] has attracted a well-paying customer. We no longer need the very special favor you have been doing for us." He said that, thanks to Shiro-chan's diligent effort, he had obtained a contract for the in-house sale of his buns at an additional movie house in Rokku. "That is certainly welcome news!" he said. "*Anpan* sell well at a movie house." Mother was truly delighted.

That night Shiro-chan called on us, her face bursting with a smile and said, "I am really grateful to you, Kato-san. I got the new contract because you encouraged me every day." She went on to explain that knowing of Mother's concern for her gave her the courage to search out a new market. Shiro-chan really looked happy. As she was leaving, she gave mother a package wrapped in newspaper and said, "This is a small token of my appreciation. Give it to O-Tei-chan and Toku-chan." The package contained five cream-filled buns. Mother and I exchanged looks of . . .

The Cherry-Blossom Actor

 "Yesterday, my husband drank too much at the cherry-blossom festival at Asukayama,⁺" the woman said. "He has a headache and can't get out of bed. I am very sorry, but could you give him a day off again?" she pleaded.

Every year, during the cherry-blossom season, this actor sent his wife to my father with this excuse. And each time, Father became angry and retorted in the same way: "I hate to say this to you, but that is why Mata-san is given only minor roles on the stage. He is a professional actor, isn't he? He should be ashamed of himself, performing with amateurs! Why can't he show that much energy on the professional stage?"

Mata-san's wife, a docile woman who would have kept staring straight ahead for three years if told to do so, kept her eyes cast down as my short-tempered father snapped abuse at her husband. She made no excuses. Father became more angry and then discouraged, feeling as if he were beating the air. Finally, he ended with a sigh, "They really depress me, both of them. But Mata is worse, he is indeed a cherry-blossom actor."

Father was right. Mata-san neglected his stage duties only once a year, for about five days in the cherry-blossom season. The rest of the year, Mata-san never

---

⁺Asukayama is a hill important for its view of the cherry blossoms and, in Sawamura's time, for its annual festival, in which local towns and districts participated in activities such as elaborate parades with amateur actors performing scenes from plays.

failed to do his duty. For that reason, my father complained, he could not fire him. At that time, I suppose,
Mata-san was over forty. He never rose beyond playing
minor roles, despite being tall and rather good-looking.
Backstage he was attentive and considerate to others and
was popular among his fellow actors. He was enthusiastic in his work, but somehow his acting was dull.
Whether he was playing a warrior or a townsman, his
lines, even when he spoke only a few words, never
impressed the audience. And the way he slouched irritated the other actors on stage.

The only time Mata-san assumed a striking pose—
actually looked like a real actor—was at the annual
parade at Asukayama. Just prior to that, he suddenly
became restless and ignored his professional stage duties
and made the excuse that he had a headache or a stomachache. From that time until its conclusion, he devoted
himself to acting alongside the amateurs at the cherry-
blossom festival.

In his Asukayama performances, Mata-san played
heroic characters, such as Oishi-Kuranosuke* or
Omatsuri-Sashichi*. So naturally he stood out among
young amateur players. Although mediocre at his craft,
he was, after all, a professional actor with a long career.
He also spent a great deal of his own money on his costumes and hair arrangement for his performance at
Asukayama. In this environment, he was successful, and
the audience out to view the cherry blossoms applauded
him enthusiastically. During that brief time, he was the
pride of his neighborhood and the center of attention.

"Ah!" my father said bitterly. "A professional actor
vying with complete amateurs!" But my mother was

sympathetic and said to me when we were alone, "Mata-san is reserved and shy by nature. He cannot act well unless he is drunk. Only at Asukayama does he have that opportunity. He is very timid, yet he likes acting so much that he cannot quit the stage. Fate can be cruel!"

The next day Mata-san mumbled his lines in the corner of the stage, with downcast eyes, as usual—he was sober, of course.

Playing in the Alleys

 In old days, children playing in the alleys of Asakusa had no toys to speak of. To play "house" they mainly used paper dolls made by their mothers with fragments of handmade paper. The dolls were in the shape of brides with the *shimada** or *marumage** hairstyles. They wore kimonos of paper adorned with colorful figures. We spread a mat under the eaves and on it arranged small unglazed clay plates and bowls our parents bought for us from night stalls* at fairs. "Please help yourself," a girl would say, offering red seeds of *aoki* [Japanese laurel] and maple leaves. "Your soup is so good," we would say, pretending to drink water in which we had soaked and squeezed morning glories for coloring. Imitating grown-ups, we exchanged such phrases and spent the whole day having fun.

Girls badgered their mothers for snippets of cloth

and with their inexperienced hands sewed them to make beanbags of unusable *adzuki* beans. These beanbags were girls' treasures. We played a game where we threw the beanbags and tried to catch two, three, and sometimes four or five with both hands. Some became quite skillful at it. The song that accompanied this game was called "Kawanakajima"*:

> Mount Saijō is deep in the mist,
> Waves are high on the Chikuma River.
> Sounds traveling from the distance,
> Are they waves or soldiers' war cries?
> The rising sun shines on the flag-bearers' hands
> Brightly, brightly, brightly.

Tomboys, taught by I don't know who, only sang the parody:

> Mount Saijō is deep in the mist
> Fish paste, fish cake and fried tofu,
> Climbing a slope is tough and rough,
> Father's head is bald and shiny,
> Slippery, slippery, slippery.

Such children's songs were not limited to Asakusa. Children all over Japan sang them. Provided with only a few toys, children made their play enjoyable by singing and talking. And the merry songs and happy games, passed on by word of mouth, spread like wildfire. From morning to evening, whenever they were together, the chatty children of Asakusa sang various songs at the top of their voices. One went like this:

For one, *Ichi*nomiya [one]
For two, the Tōshōyo-gū temple of *Ni*kkō [two]
For three, *Sa*kura-Sōgorō [three]
For four, the Zenko-ji temple of *Shi*nano [four]
For five, the Grand Shrine of *Izu*mo [five]
For six, the village's (*mu*ra) guardian god [six]
For seven, Acala, the God of Fire of *Na*rita [seven]
For eight, the Hōryu-ji temple of *Ya*mato [eight]
For nine, Saint *Kō*bō of *Kō*ya [nine]
For ten, the Sengaku-ji temple of *Ta*kanawa [ten]

Some pious old person must have composed this number song.

The song, "What Plants Do We Eat?" was about the common vegetables in our daily lives, so the rhythm of the syllables and singing it helped us learn their names: "*Ichijiku* [fig], *ni'n'ji'n* [carrot], *sa'n'sho* [Japanese pepper], ni *shiitake* [mushroom], *gobō-o* [burdock], ni *mukago* [yam], *nanakusa* [seven spring herbs], *yatsugashira* [taro], *kuko-no-mi* [a seed of a Chinese vine], *tōnasu* [pumpkin]."

A university professor born and bred in Asakusa taught me the following song, though he said his memory was uncertain:

In Kōjimachi*, elephants come out.
In Shiba, cows come out.
In Yotsuya, horses come out.
From a bell tower, a streetwalker comes out.
From the Sa'n'no Shrine, monkeys come out.

This song certainly conveys the aura of Tokyo. I

wonder how it was created. The professor says children sang it with accompanying gestures while they were walking.

Because every house was cramped, parents encouraged their children to play outdoors. Fortunately the neighborhood then had many vacant areas, such as the space around the Senso-ji temple, the garden of the Denpo-in temple, and the tea field in front of the local Flower Garden. Narrow streets divided the houses into compact blocks, and irregularly shaped lanes separated the houses that were so close to one another their eaves almost touched. The neighborhood was perfect for the children to play hide-and-seek and "compete for territory."

Another game consisted of walking down an imaginary lane. When about ten children had gathered, they lined up in two rows facing each other and extended their arms high above their heads, touching the hands of the person in front of them, thus forming an "arched roof." Then they sang a song and took turns walking under the roof. The song was "A Narrow Lane to the Tenjin Shrine," and even now children sing it:

> "Pass along, pass along."
> "Where does this lane lead to?"
> "It leads to the Tenjin Shrine."
> "Will you let me pass along?"
> "None without business shall pass."
> "I'm returning the charm for this child
> To give thanks for celebrating his seventh year."
> "Going is easy but coming back is not.
> Though not easy,

Pass along, pass along.
What gift will you offer us on your way back?"
"*Hijiki* [sweetened brown algae and soy]
   and fried tofu,
Sushi and dumplings."

If the gift nowadays is *hijiki* and dumplings, children will not allow an easy passage.

Grabbing the sash of the child in front and walking crouched in a line was called "A Rolling Caterpillar." As they ambled along they sang:

A green caterpillar is rolling, rolling.
A gourd is tumbling, tumbling.

In "Playing Streetcar," children lined up one behind another, a circle of thin string encircling them as they ran in step. "Ting-ting! A streetcar is going." That was all there was to this game, but we all ran from one alley to another and forgot the passage of time until dark. Children could buy toy scissors and red third-class play train tickets at a candy store, and the child who had them was entitled to be the conductor.

Two children often played *janken,* scissors-paper-rock. The one who won pulled up the other's sleeve and stroked, rubbed, and tickled the upper arm, saying, "*Sōmen, nyūmen, hiyasōmen, chinpi, chinpi, chinpi* [fine noodle, noodle cooked with soy sauce, iced noodles] . . ." When saying the *"chinpi"* part, the child pinched the arm harder and harder. Anyone who cried out in pain lost the game.

In a similar game, two children sang:

Otsune-san
From a Pig Dealer
From Oyster Shell Town.

If a boy and a girl played this game together, other boys who wanted to be mischievous were sure to make fun of them and shout, "Look at them. A boy and girl are parching beans. They'll never get finished" ["Parching beans" connotes intimate relations between a man and a woman]. These boys really must have wanted to join the girls and have fun.

The games boys enjoyed most were *beigoma* [spinning an iron top] and *menko*. In *beigoma*, a piece of matting was placed on a bucket or trash box to form a crater. The boys then spun their tops on this surface. The boys spun their tops with great force in order to hit others spinning in the crater. The top was named *bei* [ivory shell] *goma* [top], because the entire top, I'm told, looks like an ivory shell. A *menko* is a round piece of cardboard on which were pasted pictures of warriors. A child threw the *menko* to the ground as hard as possible, hoping to turn an opponent's *menko* upside down with the blast of air.

Both games were energetic and needed strength. Therefore, quarrels frequently arose; one child would shove or push another and they started to wrestle. Shitamachi children of those days rarely cried when hit once or twice. When a child cried occasionally, the parents ignored it and never appeared. If a mother did come out, the children would tease her child by shouting, "Look! Go get your mommy! You're a sissy. That's what you are." The mother would then be embarrassed in front of her neighbors. The children didn't need parental help. Their leader would settle the dispute fairly.

Children in the back streets enjoyed playing in the narrow corners of alleys or in vacant lots overgrown with weeds. Those were the days before television, radio, or fancy toys.

Mother and the Shobu *Bath*

These days, taking a *shobu*[+] bath at an *ofuroyo*, a place for public bathing, has become rare even in Shitamachi. But in my childhood, at Tango no Sekku, the Boys' Festival, which is celebrated on May 5, a sign was posted at the entrance of the *ofuroyo* which read "*Shobu* Bath Today." Going to the public bath on this day was a treat we all looked forward to. An even earlier custom practiced on May 5 was to fast to purify the body and avoid uncleanliness. But in my time, as I recall, Mother took me to a *shobu* bath with a prayer that we be free from any epidemic and stay in good health during the year.

On one particular Tango no Sekku, I remember Mother and I entering the dressing room and breathing in the pleasant aroma of green *shobu* which filled the air.

[+][The leaves and roots of *shobu*, sweet flag, have a sweet fragrance, and the plant is believed to ward off evil influences. For this reason, some Japanese hung a bundle of sweet flag from the house eaves.]

When four or five customers came in, the owner's wife, sitting at the entrance collecting fees, shouted in a lively voice to an employee, "Say, put in another bunch for our guests."

"OK," came an equally lively answer from near the boiler. With a splash a new bunch of *shobu* went into the bath. Crying joyfully, children jumped into the tub and scrambled to get a new green leaf.

On the draining floor surrounding the bath, some women vigorously scoured their faces and scrubbed their bodies with a small folded leaf. A *shobu* leaf was said to cure a headache if worn around the hair at the nape of the neck or, if cut in the shape of an arrow feather, inserted in the hair like an ornamental hairpin. Always an inquisitive child, I whispered to my mother, who was also rubbing her face with a leaf, "Does that really do any good?"

She looked at me with a smile and said, "I don't know. But let's keep company with the world and say that it does." Her phrase "keeping company" brought a smile to my face.

Later, in the middle of that night a great commotion arose in my house. Mother was running a high fever and one entire side of her face was swollen. She had contracted *tandoku* [St. Anthony's Fire, a serious strep infection]. She had shaved her eyebrows before going to the bath—a custom of the time, but one Mother rarely followed. As a result, the doctor said, an infection had entered from a cut above her eyelid. With his arms folded at her bedside, Father peered at Mother, who groaned in acute pain. "Uhmm. She looks like Kasane [a legendary ugly woman in a Kabuki play], she does indeed," he said, frowning like Yaemon [Kasane's husband who killed her].

Mother was laid up for about a week. On the day Mother left her bed, the wife of the bathhouse owner came to our home to see how Mother was, bringing with her a sponge cake as a get-well gift. "You got your infection from our *shobu*, didn't you? Yesterday, I heard you were sick, and my husband and I were very sorry. We don't know what to do about it." Mother replied, "Don't say that. Germs don't carry a name tag. Nobody knows how the infection entered my body. That morning, I cleared the sewage ditch. Maybe that's where the germs came from. Don't worry yourself about it." Encouraged by my mother's cheerful, laughing voice, which she had not expected, the woman left with a beaming expression.

That night, while eating the sponge cake with tea, I said, "Mother, you didn't drain the ditch that morning, did you? You got the infection from the *shobu* leaf, that's for sure."

Mother looked at me sternly and said, "Don't say that. I am also to blame; I should have been more careful. I don't want you to ever make comments that will hurt the business of our neighbors."

The following year, the *shobu* bath was also crowded when Mother and I went. On our way in she whispered, "Don't rub your face with a *shobu* leaf."

My First Serge Kimono

 Everyone in Asakusa was familiar with the Kuramae Technological College (the present Tokyo Institute of Technology), not because of its academic programs but because the school's cultural festival held an annual bazaar. This bazaar was a once-a-year opportunity to shop for luxurious and fashionable items. The wives and young girls of Shitamachi looked forward to this day and were eager for tickets. I don't know why, but in addition to selling perfume and cosmetic powder, the bazaar offered serge [a twilled, worsted fabric, used especially for clothing] cloth at a discount. In those days, serge was not widely available.

Fortunately, our family could obtain tickets every year through my aunt, a master teacher of the two-stringed *koto*. The son of one of her students attended the college, and her student gave us tickets. Because of this bazaar, my father could afford to have the first serge kimono in our family. "How comfortable it looks! It really seems genteel and neat," my mother said admiringly. The serge kimono was well-suited for the pleasant breezes of May and was smart and fashionable. Of course, my father, a dandy, was as proud as a peacock.

I seldom pestered my mother to buy anything for me. But one day when I was in my sixth grade, I confided to her that I wanted a serge kimono. She took her secret savings out of the drawer of the family altar, and we went to the college bazaar and bought the material. The serge had a modern design with thin red and white stripes running on a pale cream background. I remember how very happy I was that night as I slept with the package close to my pillow.

A few days later, with a pink ribbon in my hair and wearing my new serge kimono and a woolen sash, I went with a light heart to visit my classmate, Kamiki-san, who had invited me to her home. She was a pretty girl and the only daughter of the president of the prestigious Kamiki Bank. To tell the truth, I was in awe of her wealth and the clothes she wore. Her everyday kimono was of purple *meisen* [a silk fabric], and her red *hakama* was expensive and neatly pleated.

When I entered her mansion, I had to walk down a long, dark corridor. I almost slipped because the floor was so well polished. As I walked down the hall, I looked before me and almost cried out in surprise. A girl, dressed in a kimono of the same design as mine, was walking toward me. She seemed stuck-up and had an affected gait. "She has a kimono just like mine, the same pattern and everything," I thought. I immediately disliked her. As we approached, I was a bit angry and stepped to my right to let her pass. As I did so, she stepped in the same direction. When I stepped to my left, she did too. We came closer, almost bumping into each other.

Then it hit me—I was looking at my own image in the mirror that covered the entire wall at the end of the corridor. I was so relieved. A huge grin spread across my face. The other "me" grinned, too.

"What's keeping you, O-Tei-chan? Come quick this way," said Kamiki-san, coming from a back room. She led me into a large room jutting out over the Sumida River. Her mother, a gentle, beautiful woman, welcomed me with a smile and said, "How nice you look in that kimono!"

Just like my father, I was as proud as a peacock and drew a deep breath as I faced the cooling wind that came over the waters.

The Doctor Killer

 Even now, when May approaches, I thrill at the thought of eating the season's first bonito. I attribute this feeling to my father. He was a great gourmet and frequently uttered the popular saying of the day, that he would "pawn his wife to eat the first bonito of the season." Thick, tender slices of raw bonito are exquisite and seem to melt on the tongue. The Tosa folk cuisine dish of lightly roasted bonito, *tataki,* is equally delicious. A homemade dish of an entire fillet of bonito skewered on an iron spit and quickly roasted is excellent too, especially when served with chopped green onions and grated ginger.

Economical as she was, Mother was creative in preparing bonito and took advantage of almost every part of the fish. After she removed the best part of the meat for sashimi, she seasoned the rest bittersweet to make these leftovers more attractive. Mother was particularly inventive with the backbone which had chunks of meat clinging to it. Although it was nourishing and not unpleasant tasting, she had a difficult task in persuading me to eat it. Mother chopped the backbone into irregular pieces and boiled them along with thin slices of ginger. Then she skillfully picked off the blood-colored meat between the bones. When she was finished, she urged me to eat it. I recall her saying, "To tell the truth, this is the best part. It is good for an anaemic child like you." Because of her effort and because it was Mother, I accepted her ploy.

When she had eaten all of the edible parts, Mother added hot water to the seasoned gravy that remained and offered this "soup" to me. She called it the "doctor killer." When I first heard this phrase, I asked, "Why on earth does it have such a strange name?" She smiled knowingly and replied, "Because it makes people so healthy that doctors don't have any more patients. Then they must go out of business." Although I was a delicate child, I hardly ever saw a doctor, perhaps because of the "doctor killer" bonito soup I used to eat. Even now, after I have eaten bonito boiled firm in soy sauce, I follow my mother's advice and eat the "doctor killer." I keep it a secret, though, because it seems a bit uncouth to eat it.

The Nigenkin
*and the Belle of Nakamise**

 A master of the *nigenkin*[+] appears in Natsume Sōseki's novel *I Am a Cat.* She is described as "the daughter of a nephew of the mother-in-law of a sister of the secretary who served Tenshoin." This explanation of a girl's social status was so roundabout and amusing that I burst out laughing when I first read it.

My aunt, my father's younger sister, was a master of the *nigenkin.* She was the mistress of an aristocratic descendent of a feudal lord and lived at Denmacho in Asakusa. Her house was stylish and surrounded by a fence of black boards. Later she became the headmaster of the prestigious Azuma School* of this *koto* and as such inherited the name of the founder, Rosen Tosha IV. Her playing was so accomplished, I am told, that people who passed her house stopped outside the fence and listened, charmed by the beautiful, clear sounds of her music.

When I was a little child, I took lessons from her together with my elder sister, whom my aunt had adopted and who lived with her. The *nigenkin* was sleek and easy to carry, and when placed on its stand with carved legs, it was the height of a table, about knee high.

[+]A *nigenkin* is a two-stringed *koto,* a shorter and narrower variation of the traditional thirteen-string zither-like instrument made of wood from the Japanese paulownia tree. The *nigenkin* is long and slender, about five inches wide and slightly over three feet long, and played in a sitting position.

A *koto* player determines the pitch by pressing the strings with a thick ivory ring, a *rokan**, worn on the middle finger of the left hand. The notes are played by plucking the two purple strings with a pick, or plectrum, worn on the right index finger. A proper performance is very graceful. The sound of a *nigenkin* is similar to that of the traditional *koto* or the *shamisen**, another popular stringed instrument—somewhat metallic, thin, high-pitched, and refined. Perhaps because of the elegance of the instrument, girls from well-to-do families in Shitamachi began to take lessons in the *nigenkin*.

At this time, one of my aunt's favorite pupils was Chieko-san, whose family owned a long-established Nakamise store, which sold various kinds of purses and pouches. I recall my aunt saying, "Chieko-san has a natural aptitude for the *nigenkin*. She is bright and even-tempered. Above all, she is attractive and is a pleasure to look at." My aunt, who had a high standard for everything, praised Chieko-san without reserve.

Once, when I was five or six, I recall peeping from behind a screen to watch Chieko-san take her lesson. I still remember clearly the throbbing excitement of the sight. Chieko-san wore a printed silk kimono with a striped sash and had a decorative silver pin in her heavy *shimada* hairdo. She must have been seventeen or eighteen. Her unpainted white, round cheeks were slightly flushed, and her small unrouged lips were bright and red. With her head lowered slightly, she played the *nigenkin* intently. The sight was as beautiful as a watercolor print, and I gave a small sigh, mere child as I was. My sister whispered from behind: "Everyone talks about her. They call her the 'Belle of Nakamise.'"

Her family's shop displayed purses and tobacco pouches made of *inden* [sheepskin or deerskin], *shobugawa* [deerskin with iris dyed on an indigo background], printed cotton, and *tozan* [a finely woven cotton fabric with a lustrous finish and usually vertical stripes]. Chieko-san usually wore a yellow-striped kimono with a black neckband and an apron, her sleeves tucked up with a red cord. As customers passed on Nakamise's stone pavement, Chieko-san, with a sweet smile and her head slightly tilted to one side, called softly, "Please come in and look around." Few people passed without stopping. Not a few young men visited her shop every day instead of the Kannon temple. She was literally the shop's main attraction.

As I have been told, for only two hours, around midnight, the Nakamise quarters of Asakusa were completely devoid of the sounds of people passing. Chieko-san's shop opened at six in the morning and closed at ten at night, so tending the shop during that time must have been heavy work for a young girl. Recalling those days, Chieko-san said that even in midwinter she had only a small coal heater to warm her hands, hardly big enough for the purpose. With her *nigenkin* lessons as her only diversion, Chieko-san continued to work in the shop. She performed this duty, supported by the thought that she was helping her elder brother in his studies because their father had died. Although heir to the family business, her brother did not like owning the shop and was studying at the Medical School of Tokyo University. Unfortunately, her brother, the hope of his grandmother, mother, and Chieko, died suddenly soon after graduation.

When she was twenty, Chieko-san married a young

show manager of the Rokku area of Asakusa. He was reputed to be a very capable man in his business. My mother knew Chieko-san well and liked her. When she saw her, a new wife and beautiful as a flower, Mother said happily, "Chieko-san will surely lead a happy life now." Only my aunt complained because her beloved pupil stopped coming for her lessons.

I'm not sure how long it was, but several years later, Chieko-san resumed her lessons and practiced even more seriously than she had before her marriage. During these years, I had heard, her husband, who was a very talented manager in the theaters and movie houses of Rokku, had had numerous love affairs. I recall hearing a friend say, "Just think how he wooed her because of her beauty. Now look what he is doing! This is too much! Chieko-san is miserable!" Her friends were exasperated and angry. But somehow Chieko-san seemed unconcerned by their comments. She said, "Working with extravagant theater people often puts a man in tempting situations. I suppose this is the case with my husband. I just have to close my eyes to some things." True to her word, she never complained or reproached him.

✦ ✦ ✦

Chieko-san is over eighty now. And because of her musical excellence, she has been awarded the name Rosui Tosha. Her skill in the *nigenkin* was designated an "Intangible Cultural Property" by the Japanese government some time ago and is treasured in the world of traditional Japanese music. Now she arranges her white hair casually in a bun at the back of her neck, and her smooth cheeks, on which I hear she never applied make-up, have not a single spot: she is as beautiful as a doll of the old wife of *Takasago**. More than once, I have heard her say, "I have experienced many hardships in my life, but women of the older generation like me were taught to endure. Making a fuss would not have helped."

When I visited her at her home in Kyodo after a long interval, Chieko-san was in a good humor. She took out her *nigenkin* and played a traditional Japanese song, "Kogo*," a tragic story of a young lady-in-waiting from the *Tale of Heike*. The notes were clear in suggesting a woman's sorrow which rests deep in her heart. Thanks to her, I took great pleasure in this quiet afternoon—something I had not done for a very long time. During this time, her husband, who was also quite old, seemed to be enjoying his tea in the back room. "These days," she said, "he never leaves me." Then she turned to me and whispered, smiling at me with her eyes as clear as those of a little girl: "I suppose living alone would be less demanding."

On Makeup

 Asakusa women from respectable households rarely used cosmetics. Living where they did, they saw women from the theater district every day. But they never envied nor scorned these women for their overly thick makeup and garish red rouge. The occupation required it. The Asakusa women therefore thought that applying *hechima no mizu,* a lotion made from the sap of a common garden gourd, to their faces was good enough for those who didn't rely on their personal beauty for a living. They didn't want any conflicting odors to detract from the subtle aroma of the *miso* soup they made.

The men of Asakusa also preferred that their wives and daughters refrain from using makeup. Yet these same men flagrantly caroused with the overly made-up women who worked in the district. Was it that the men had enough of the smell of makeup outside their homes and did not want it brought inside? Or were they leery of other men trifling with their wives and daughters?

If young girls used too much rouge and powder in the daytime, except for the Bon Festival* or New Year holidays, I often heard their fathers chastise them: "Silly girl! It's broad daylight, the time when proper ghosts have long vanished. Take a cake of soap, go to the public bath, and wash your face!"

The Sanja Festival

 [Every Shinto shrine, such as the Asakusa Shrine (Sanja-sama)* has one or more *mikoshi,* portable shrines in which a god sits. *Mikoshi* vary in size and have a square base, typically one to two square meters. They are supported by bars and carried at the shrine's festival and represent the god touring the district and receiving devotion from area residents. The Sanja-sama had four *mikoshi,* the fourth being the largest.] When I was a young girl, everyone looked forward to the Sanja Festival with more enthusiasm than they had for the Bon Festival or the New Year. As May 17 and 18 approached, all Asakusa suddenly came to life. The main festival alternated yearly with the lesser, or "shadow," festival. At the latter, groups of young people carried three ornate and beautifully made *mikoshi*—the *ichi-no-miya* [number-one shrine], the *ni-no-miya* [number-two shrine], and the *san-no-miya* [number- three shrine]. These *mikoshi,* however, were subdued, that is, they did not cause much commotion.

On the other hand, when the *shi-no-miya,* the number-four shrine, was added at the main festival, it was said that the mounting excitement sometimes resulted in actual bloodshed. This shrine, far larger and heavier than any of the other three, was borne on the shoulders of energetic young men, in particular those who took pride in their strength and muscles. They beat their chests with their fists and boasted to others: "Hey! The *shi-no-miya* is too heavy for you, you scrawny weaklings. Get out of our way. Leave it to us." With admiring looks, small boys watched them pass and thought, "Oh, how I want to carry the *shi-no-miya* when I grow up."

"Heave ho! Heave ho!" the young men shouted as they shoved and pushed with all their might. Their *hachimaki* [headbands symbolizing their determination] were tied tightly around their heads, and the *happi* and *pacchi* [short coats and pure-white trousers] of their uniforms were soaked with sweat. When thirsty, they grabbed a dipper and gulped down saké with style and gusto from a *shitodaru* [a twenty-gallon barrel] containing the offering to the gods. Each district proudly paraded with its own *mikoshi*. Someone might say, "Let's ram our *mikoshi* into the *shi-no-miya* this year." Having had too much to drink, they would clash if their shrine touched, or even slightly evaded, another. Over such trivialities, they actually provoked fights. Naturally some got hurt, for they were young, hot-tempered, and full of vigor.

Be that as it may, the morning after the festival, no one seemed to recall the fights. No one held a grudge against a person who hit, or even injured, him. Such fights were, so to speak, outlets for the overflowing energy of young men. All involved in the fights were Edoites, nowadays called Tokyoites—careless, restless, and without guile. The morning after the festival, it was as if a soft summer rain had washed away all memory of the violence of the previous night. So from the outset, their elders were not worried. It was all part of the festival.

Each year was the same—the community leaders spared no expense in making elaborate kimonos and *nagajuban* [the long garments worn beneath kimonos], while children scampered in identical cotton kimonos, tucking their sleeves with flax cords from which large jingling bells hung as they had traditionally done. Young girls with their hair beautifully arranged and dressed neatly in fresh kimonos and wearing new *geta* [wooden clogs] were cheerful from morning until night. But they were always busy! They had to get the saké ready for the men, boil vegetables with soy, prepare *okowa* [steamed glutinous rice] with red beans, and boil green soybeans in such a way as not to spoil their color. It was enough to make your head spin.

At the sounds of shouting and cheering in the streets, girls would cry, "Here comes the *mikoshi!*" But the most they could do was lay aside *kon'nyaku** cooking in the pan, run out, and lift themselves on tiptoes. If a girl inadvertently peeped from a window of the second story, she would be shouted at, "You're a brazen, obnoxious girl to look down on the *mikoshi!*" If by chance a girl touched one, what a fuss would result! Someone would shout, "A girl touched a *mikoshi!* It has been desecrated. Bring some salt and purify it, quick!" They would give her a terrible time.

✦ ✦ ✦

Last year, I went to see the Sanja Festival after an interval of some thirty-odd years. Involuntarily I whispered, "Surely equal rights have arrived." I saw a number of young girls amid the men carrying the *mikoshi.* I choked with emotion at the sight. The girls seemed to be hanging from the bars rather than carrying the shrine. At any rate, they were touching a *mikoshi,* each wearing the same kind of *happi* the men wore, the same kind of *hachimaki* with a spotted pattern tied round her head, the same kind of tight-fitting *pacchi,* and the same kind of hemp-soled straw sandals. Their fresh young skin with no makeup was flushed, their rouged lips stood out, their temples streamed with sweat. They were really lovely and beautiful! The sight made me extremely happy. Oh, I wished that I could have done that.

But I wondered if the young men who carried the *mikoshi,* as if protecting the girls, seemed as dashing as before. In the past, their roughness, their open display of masculinity, during the festival made young girls' hearts throb when they peeped from the kitchen window. Are the boys weaker now that the girls have become stronger, have become their equals? No, no, that is not the case, I bet. Yet, the festivals have become less popular with young people. Perhaps with so many diversions available everywhere all year round, diversions more entertaining than the festival, people in general no longer look forward to the following year's festival with enthusiasm.

✦ ✦ ✦

I have been told that the *shi-no-miya,* the violent *mikoshi,* was not rebuilt after it was destroyed in an air raid during the last war.

Kon'nichi-sama, the Spirit of the New Day

 "Asakusa women of our generation wear well indeed!" I said, laughing involuntarily and filled with warm nostalgia and surprise. It was the night of the Sanja Festival, and after fifty years, two of my primary school classmates were before me in an upstairs room at the home of Mr. Yoshikawa, a close friend of my older brother. Such a long time had passed since we were twelve or thirteen and had "just started our lives." Now in a leap of time, we were sixty-five or - six, "nearing the end of our lives." But the two still retained their former appearance and looked young.

They share the same first name, O-Taka-san, so, when either was called in school, they frequently answered together. The shorter O-Taka-san's father sold clog thongs, and she married into a family that owned an artificial flower shop. She attended to the needs of the craftsmen working for the shop and also cared for her mother-in-law, a strong-minded woman. I had been told that after the long years of the war, she lost her husband and suffered all kinds of hardships. Yet, except for some fine wrinkles on her forehead and white hair on her temples, which we all have, her natural fair skin was more smooth and bright than when she was a girl. She was neatly dressed in a very subdued, pin-striped kimono, and the brisk way she carried herself was a delight to the eye.

The father of the taller O-Taka-san sold poultry, and she now runs a fine restaurant. The food is tasty yet inexpensive, and the restaurant is always full. Her homemade pickles are unequaled. Her secret is her attention to detail: She rises in the middle of night and pickles vegetables so that her customers can eat them at just the right time. This O-Taka-san is gently stout, just as she was as a child. All year round, she bustles about her restaurant, often holding up the sleeves of her kimono with a makeshift *tasuki* [a cord women used for this purpose because of the bulk of their sleeves] of stray pieces of paper string she picked up. Her good-natured face is slightly flushed as she smiles happily, her eyes half-closed.

"Women of our days worked constantly, yet even now, they look as young as ever. Does this mean that by working hard they have been getting the proper amount of exercise? I wonder," I said, tilting my head in thought. Yukiyo-san, Mr. Yoshikawa's wife, had just prepared some festive red rice and boiled vegetables and was dishing it out for us on small plates. She laughed and said, "In a way, they have been doing calisthenics all these years." Yukiyo-san is about our age and is tall and lean; she moves briskly and is always cheerful. She had attended a pharmacy college, a rarity for an Asakusa girl, but her life after her marriage seems to have been as full of hardships as ours.

As they listened to us praise their youthful appearance, the two O-Taka-sans were embarrassed and exchanged glances. The taller one finally said, "Calisthenics or labor, I must work as long as I'm alive; otherwise I'll be punished for ignoring the blessings I enjoy." "That's right," the shorter one added. "I can't be lazy; if I am, I'll be ungrateful to Kon'nichi-sama."

My mother also used to speak of Kon'nichi-sama. Every night, while going to bed exhausted, she murmured, "Resting in bed is heaven, and only fools of the weary world get up and work." Yet at the break of dawn, she tied up her sleeves with a *tasuki* and hurried to the kitchen. When I asked her why she worked so hard, she used to say, "I cannot justify being lazy to Kon'nichi-sama."

Nobody knows where Kon'nichi-sama is enshrined

or whether it is a god or a Buddha. Though they did not say it explicitly, in the past, honest women used to think that, each day, as long as they were not ill, they must never be idle; otherwise they would be shamed before "someone." This "someone" they called "Kon'nichi-sama." So they never complained even when their hard work produced no tangible results. Looking as easy-going as ever, the shorter O-Taka-san said, "Nobody wants to listen to your grumblings."

As we were about to say goodbye, the taller O-Taka-san hesitantly said, "I have one worry, only one, that bothers me." She said she was very happy that her youngest son was going to marry a very nice girl, but O-Taka-san wondered if she would have to avoid working as hard as she had always done. When they lived together, would her daughter-in-law resent her rising in the middle of night to pickle vegetables? "But when I think of my customers, I don't want to stop the practice," she said plaintively. She seemed at a loss. The way she put her hand to her plump cheek made her look as naive and sweet as she did when she was a little girl.

Pray, Kon'nichi-sama, give your kind assistance to this girl!

Koromogae, the Seasonal Changing of Clothing

 In former days the upper-class society had fastidious rules about seasonal changes of dress, such as beginning to wear lined kimonos on April 1 of the lunar calendar, unlined kimonos on May 5, and raw silk garments on August 15. In my childhood the people of Shitamachi retained this seasonal custom in June and October.

On the day of *koromogae,* Mother bustled about busily beginning at early morning. She replaced the paper-covered *shoji,* the sliding doors, of the entrance hall and those on the second story with *shoji* made of reed and brought out fans and mosquito-repellant incense. These changes made it seem like summer inside our small house. Then mother took out the family's summer kimonos from the wicker baskets in which they had been stored in closets during the winter and put this summer wear in our *tansu,* the chests of drawers that held our everyday clothing. When she had packed our winter garments, our cotton-quilted clothing and lined kimonos, in the wicker baskets and replaced them in the closets, our *koromogae* was finished. This was all there was to it. But for Mother it was an important yearly event.

From my childhood I was sensitive to heat, and as early as the latter part of May, I perspired along my hair-line and under my arms. But I endured the heat, accepting that I had to wear my heavy lined kimono until the day of *koromogae.* Then, changing into an unlined kimono at long last, I felt relief. But soon the rainy season set in, bringing chilly days. On such days I again put on a *haori*, a lined short jacket, and remained huddled by the reed door. In spite of such inconveniences, my family strictly observed *koromogae*, almost to the point of being stubborn about it.

When I think of this custom today, I am reminded of an incident involving a dear family friend, Kazuhei-san, who used to visit our house regularly when I was a child. He was nearly fifty years old then and was an attendant for a leading Kabuki actor. He had many children and, because of his tight household finances, always wore the same cotton kimono, the attire provided by his master. As I recall, it had a Kinokuni pattern, a kind of checkered pattern. Whenever Kazuhei-san came by, Mother handed him some money out of her secret savings, which she kept in the drawer of the family altar.

On the last day of May (I forget the year), Kazuhei-san dropped by, but Mother happened to be out. For a moment, he looked quite confused, then left. The next day, when she had finished her chores related to *koromogae* and was resting, Kazuhei-san again appeared. At one point, he said, "Every household is busy today with *koromogae*. This is our tradition so we must observe it without fail. In my home too, my wife is busy making a mess. We are Edoites, aren't we?"

When Mother rose to go to the family altar to get some money for him, Kazuhei-san, seated at the edge of the room with his knees together, produced a tobacco pouch from his sleeve. He wore his usual checkered kimono, but I noticed that it was now unlined. Looking more closely, I saw a few threads hanging from the end of his sleeves. Apparently, the night before, his wife had removed the lining and, in her haste, forgot to stitch the seam.

Every year, when the season progresses from spring to early summer, the time of *koromogae*, I recall the lean shoulders of Kazuhei-san shivering that day in an unlined kimono.

Recollections of O-Fuji-sama Fairs

 Every year when I see irises arranged in a vase in the *tokonoma* [the alcove in the best room of the house, next to which guests tradition- ally sit], I am reminded of iris dumplings. When I was a child, it was a treat to buy them at an O-Fuji-sama fair. A bamboo stick as thick as a *saibashi* [the large chopsticks used for serving food] was split length- wise into fourths, and each of these had four red-and-white dumplings the size of prayer beads skewered on it. The small dumplings roasted over charcoal and dipped in molasses looked like irises. This is but one of my fond recollections of O-Fuji-sama fairs. These fairs were held four days each year (May 31, June 1, June 30, and July 1) and honored the deities of Mount Fuji, Asama-Gongen*. In fact, O-Fuji-sama became the popular name for the shrine in Asakusa at Kisakata-machi.

June 1 is also the opening day of the climbing season at Mount Fuji. I am told that on this day devout believers of Asakusa who could not climb Mount Fuji on a pilgrimage used to clothe themselves in white and pray while purifing themselves with cold water. But to me, ever since I was old enough to remember, June 1 was the fair when adults and children enjoyed strolling among the booths in their summer kimonos and *geta* [wooden clogs].

I recall holding a skewer of iris dumplings in each hand, taking bites first from one and then from the other and running to the booth that sold *kobaiyaki*, crackers shaped like plum flowers. A miniature shrine was at the booth, and when a one-*sen* coin was dropped into the slot next to a small door on the shrine, a bell rang, the door opened, and a toy rat popped out with a piece of paper in its mouth—a piece of paper telling our fortune. Children found this device more fascinating than the crackers and offered many *sen* to the shrine.

Once when I was seven or eight years old and it was particularly humid at the O-Fuji-sama fair, I asked our favorite stall keeper, Roku-san, for a bowl of *yosenabi*, a chowder of rice-flour pastry. He shook his head and said, "No, little girl, this weather isn't good for eating chowder. Get *tada-shinko* instead." He handed me a wood shaving as thick as a postcard holding dabs of white, red, blue, and yellow rice paste. "Making various things at home with this is fun. I'm afraid that eating suspicious foods on such a humid day may upset your stomach." I thought then that he was a strange man to tell me that something he was selling was "suspicious." But he was likeable, with small, kind eyes, so I followed his advice.

That same night, Hajime, the boy who lived next

door, was sick with diarrhea, and the whole neighborhood was quite concerned, fearing he had children's
dysentery. However, we soon discovered the real cause
of his disorder. It seemed that he had eaten too many
"ice dumplings," balls of shaved ice rolled hard like a
rice ball with red or yellow syrup poured on them.
Hajime had eaten five of them! When the commotion
was over, I said to my mother, "The man who sells 'ice
dumplings' didn't tell Hajime-san that eating too many
would give him an upset stomach, did he?" My mother
laughed and said, "Of course not. His business is selling
them." The thought that Roku-san lost business by not
selling me what I had asked for worried me. In those
days the children of Asakusa, to varying degrees, owed
much to the kind Roku-san.

But the O-Fuji-sama fair didn't just appeal to children. The garden plant section was particularly enjoyable for grown-ups. Fuji Alley, from the back of the park
to the precincts of the shrine, was lined with stalls selling garden plants and was lit by carbide lamps hung
next to the stalls. At the front of each were beautifully
displayed pots of *tokonatsu* [China pink] with pretty red
flowers, purple *kikyo* [Chinese bellflowers], *urashima*,
said to bloom for a hundred days, white *suisen* [daf-
fodils], *sasa* [small-size bamboo grass], and small *momiji*
[maple trees]. Behind them stood *aoki* [Japanese lau-
rels], *yatsude**, and slender pines with their roots bound
with straw rope.

My father, who loved flowers, squatted before the
array at one stall and examined the flowers carefully.
Then he turned to the vendor and asked, "How much

will you charge for those three—this *nadeshiko* [fringed pink] and the white and the purple *kikyo*?" The vendor paused and looked at Father for a moment and responded: "You're a regular customer. I'll sell them to *you* for one hand [fifty-*sen*]." Father shook his head and smiled and said, "Come on! You look like a helpful guy, but you charge too much. How about this?" and he held up three fingers, meaning thirty *sen*. The vendor nodded, "Okay, you win. You are the first customer today, so I'll go down to four." "Come down a little more," Father said.

Tired of waiting for the conclusion of this haggling, I looked behind me to find the fish dealer's son squatting and gazing at a potted maple tree he held in his hand. A fish dealer is usually exuberant and cheerful, yet his mother had often complained to the neighborhood women that her son was too shy and gentle to follow in his father's trade. "My son is twenty-five, yet he is afraid to hold a girl's hand. Something is wrong with him. I'm worried."

The young man seemed to be interested in buying the potted tree, but he just squatted and never moved. Smoking silently, the old dealer watched him. Suddenly in a patter of footsteps, a young girl in a colorful summer kimono appeared and, almost out of breath, stood beside the young man. He quickly stood up and exchanged smiles with the girl. Then the two walked away shoulder to shoulder. I had never seen him look so cheerful and manly. The small potted maple tree he had been gazing at lay on its side. The vendor picked it up and, dusting dirt off its small branches, smiled with resignation.

The O-Fuji-sama fair was a treat for children, grownups, and young people as well.

Acquiring Polite Accomplishments

 Growing up in Asakusa, I often heard someone say, "On June 6 of a girl's sixth year, begin lessons in music, singing, or dancing. That most surely assures her advancement." I wonder if this tradition was handed down only in Shitamachi. In Asakusa, both wealthy dry goods merchants, who had their shops on the main streets, and craftsmen, who lived a hand-to-mouth life on the back streets, took their six-year-old daughters to dancing schools or *shamisen* teachers and paid the prescribed fee. The girls played the *shamisen,* their bodies almost leaning over the instrument, which was too big to hold on their small knees, and chanted the lyrics of a song frequently used in teaching beginners: *"Yoi-i ya-a ma-a chi-i . . ."* [*Yoi wa machi,* that is "waiting in the rain"]. Or on the dancing stage, they played the role of Fujimusume*, shaking their heads and posing coquettishly, all the while held from behind by the teacher.

Girls of six, actually, four or five, if their ages were counted as we do today[†] could hardly have been expected to have enjoyed such lessons. While waiting as

---

[†]See "kazoe-doshi" in Glossary.

others before them took their lessons, they diverted themselves with childish games, such as guessing the color of the pattern of another's sleeve which they covered with their hands. I wonder why parents were so eager to have their children take those lessons. The only time my mother ever spanked me hard occurred when she discovered that I had secretly skipped my *nagauta** music lesson. Indeed many parents believed that skills in one or two kinds of music or in dancing were necessary accomplishments for a woman.

However, mothers who eked out tuition payments for their daughters' lessons from their scanty savings may have had a more serious purpose in mind: "When my daughter marries, her husband may die young, or he may be unfaithful and desert her. If she is well trained in music or dancing, she might make a living by teaching. Even if, as bad luck would have it, she must become a geisha, she would earn more money if she is a good musician or dancer."

Am I going too far if I say that this "women's wisdom" was a prudent choice in the days when a woman had no other way to make a living than to teach music or entertain men? At any rate, social conditions were quite different from those of today when children are asked to take piano or violin lessons only to please their parents. Perhaps this tradition for six-year-old girls was peculiar to Shitamachi.

My Nagauta* *Music Teacher*

 A narrow back street branching from the main street before the Miyato Theater led to a *nagauta** school where I learned to sing lyrical songs accompanied by the *shamisen.* The teacher was a cheerful, fair-skinned, stout woman. But her voice was hoarse, and she sang the high notes with difficulty, sticking her chin up. To me, who was then a little child, she seemed an older woman—thirty-four or -five—but she may have been much younger.

Like other Asakusa teachers, she never minced words when scolding her pupils. Yet her eyes were sweet and good-natured. Housewives in the neighborhood spoke well of her and said, "She is a woman of strong character and takes good care of her mother." As a result, her small school was always crowded with young pupils. I had heard that to take care of her sickly mother, she had been earning a living since she was a young woman— with only her *shamisen.* I recall occasionally seeing a small, thin old woman come out of the kitchen, but she seemed nervous and gloomy and never talked to us children.

Living upstairs in the same house was a young man, who I heard was my teacher's distant relative. He had thick eyebrows and a rather large, determined mouth. He looked twenty-three or -four, and apparently was an artist who painted in the Japanese style. A friend who was learning to become a geisha told me our teacher said, "He is an artist," then added, "or a would-be artist." She whispered: "One of my more experienced friends told me that he is really our teacher's lover." That reminded me of something I had noticed. Whenever the teacher heard the man walking down the stairs, she became anxious. Her eyes followed him until he had finished doing whatever he had come down for and had gone back to his room. She did not scold me in her usual manner even when I, sitting at the music stand right in front of her, played the wrong notes on the *shamisen*. I guess she wasn't listening.

One day during the rainy season when the sky was particularly threatening and my teacher was giving a lesson, her face seemed as clouded as the sky. Across the room, her old mother, lips trembling and looking as if she were about to collapse, was scrubbing the corridor with a dry cloth. Just then the "would-be" artist slowly came down the stairs and, without even glancing at our teacher, slid open the front door, rattling it in his haste, and went out. How sad my teacher looked! Her eyes were fixed on the man's retreating figure even as she sang the lesson. Her thick round shoulders hung limp, and her face was pale. I could not bear to look at her. "The stronger a woman's character, the more trouble she has with a man," I recalled my mother saying, mere child that I was.

The next day the sunny weather returned after a long interval. And once again, my teacher seemed cheerful—as if she had completely shed the previous day's sorrow. And once again she scolded us relentlessly. When I left that day, her mother was still in the kitchen. But the "artist's" clogs were placed neatly in the cabinet at the door.

My Red-Thonged Hiyori

Washing my family's clogs had been my household chore since I was a very young girl. In those days the streets of Shitamachi were poor, and even a brief shower turned them into muddy paths. When the rainy season set in with a continual drizzle day after day, our *ashida* [high clogs used in bad weather] and *hiyori* [low, fair-weather clogs] were always muddy.

On the occasional bright day during the rainy season, when the sun shed its rays on the glass of our *koshido,* the latticed front door, I was always busy. I brought all the clogs outside and, changing the water in a large bucket many times, scrubbed them with a dustcloth to wash off the mud. I had to do this task quickly because the streets were exposed to the sun for only a short time. By the side of the front door was a window one *ken* [almost two meters] wide, under which was a low bamboo fence. After washing the clogs, I hung one on top of each bamboo stake to dry.

One day toward evening, when I was in my fifteenth *kazoe** year, I was taking in the clogs that I had hung on the fence to dry that morning. I noticed that my *hiyori* were missing. They were old, and I had changed the wooden pieces that gave them their height many times. So I didn't regret the loss. Yet I was puzzled. Strange! I had certainly put out my clogs, the ones with red thongs, with the others. It was impossible that someone had stolen them because right next to them were my father's brand-new *ashida.* "You weren't careful enough, were you?" my mother complained. When I went to bed, I was still in a bad mood.

The next morning when I stepped down to the dirt floor at the entrance to unlock the door, I noticed a square white envelope inserted near the base of the lattice as if to conceal it from passersby. There was no sender's name or address. I was about to call my mother but paused—thinking about the loss of my clogs the day before. Mother was chopping pickles in the kitchen, and neither my father nor older brother were up yet. Quietly, I opened the envelope. The letter was addressed to me and said: "I always watch you from a distance. I love you. Will you please see me." It continued in the same vein—three pages of stationery written closely in small characters in good handwriting. It concluded, "I will wait for you under the five-storied pagoda in the park from seven to nine o'clock every night. You don't know me, but you will recognize your *hiyori* with the red thongs, which I will be holding." Then I knew—the writer of this letter had taken my clogs.

As a girl of fifteen I did not know what to do about my first love letter. Who could he be? Was he playing a joke? But if he were serious . . . The thought frightened and embarrassed me so much that I could not even tell my mother. I immediately hid the letter deep in my kimono near my heart. Did he know that I slept in the room near the entrance? That I opened the *koshido* every morning? Did he know all such details? Every morning, for an entire week, he placed love letters in the lattice of the door.

I began to imagine that each morning he would again

place a white envelope at the door. A young man I did not know, sneaking up to the door late at night, inserting his letter . . . Just the thought of it kept me awake! Every night, if I heard a noise at the door, my eyes popped. But I didn't have the courage to get up and see. Every night, I prayed, "Please stop doing this." But every day, I found an envelope there in the morning. My mother noticed my despondency and asked what was wrong. I felt I had no choice but to lie, so once I told her I had a cold, and another time I said I had a headache.

On the eighth morning, I was greatly relieved when I found no envelope. I never learned who sent the letters. For after the first letter, I burned all the rest in our stove without ever opening them. To a young girl who was like a green apple, having no idea what it meant to be in love, this experience was embarrassing and burdensome.

Seeing me suddenly regain my appetite, my mother said, "Oh, you've shaken off your cold, have you?"

"Yes, Mother. Completely."

"I bet the *shoga-yu* [a drink made with hot water and ginger] you had last night must have done it. Shall I make you another tonight?"

"No, thanks. I'm all right now," I smiled and ate another bowl of *miso* soup.

Three days later, I was feeling like my old self as I opened the door in the morning. I was shocked by what I saw—sitting neatly before the door were my old *hiyori* with red thongs. Seeing them made me shudder. The clogs with their limp red thongs seemed to stare at me as if pleading! I stared back and said to myself: "It's not my fault! Really, it is not! You had no right to say those things to me!" Finally I picked up the clogs and gently pushed them under a pile of rubbish.

✦ ✦ ✦

To this day, I believe that those clogs hindered me in learning about love!

Mother's Marumage *⁺* *Hairstyle*

 As a child I enjoyed seeing my mother having her hair done on the porch. The hairdresser wore a broad apron with splashed patterns and her sleeves tucked up with a cord. I watched her intently, combing and straightening my mother's long hair, her busy fingers glistening with oil. The aroma of hair oil floated in the air. With her eyes closed, Mother sat comfortably before an old-fashioned round mirror that stood on collapsible legs. A slight smile played about her mouth, and her face seemed relaxed. For her, busy from morning to night, this hour of hairdressing must have been a pleasant respite.

In those days a hairdresser visited houses in turn, every five days, as I recall, for the wives in Asakusa had

---

⁺The *marumage* was a married woman's hairstyle, with a single, round chignon. According to *Memories of Silk and Straw* by Junichi Saga (Kodansha International, 1987), the *marumage* chignon symbolizes the unity of a woman's heart with her husband's (152). The *obako* was the hairstyle worn by old women or widows in mourning. See Glossary.

no time to go to the shop. Clattering her arrival with her low clogs, she would come to the kitchen door and call in a high-pitched voice, "Hellooo! Is it convenient now?" My mother would routinely respond, "I've been expecting you. Come in, please." Mother cheerfully put away her sewing articles and spread a thin matting on the floor of the porch. At that time her hair was dressed in the *marumage* style.

In a folding paper case, which the hairdresser handled with care, were her tools—fine-toothed combs for removing dandruff, small combs for brushing up the sides, combs for tidying the hairline, paper cords for tying the hair. The hairdresser used these tools skillfully and did Mother's hair quickly. She tied it with a blue band, which suited mother well. "Your fine hair makes my working on it worthwhile," she said. Although habitual, her compliments seemed genuine.

"You flatter me," Mother said, embarrassed, but she seemed happy all the same and spent some time, after the hairdresser left, looking at her self in the mirrors set against each other. "I'm dark-skinned and homely," she must have thought to herself. For Mother believed herself to be plain, an unlikely match for my father. I now think that her long black hair was her only feature she was proud of. She did not use cosmetics but took good care of her hair by washing it with *funori* seaweed and flour boiled in water. However busy she was, Mother never declined her hairdresser's call. To my child's eyes, watching my mother with her hair arrayed in the *marumage* style was a genuine pleasure.

✦ ✦ ✦

One morning when I was about nine, I woke up to find Mother crouched before the kitchen sink, stripped to her waist and washing her hair. I was puzzled. Just the day before she had had her hair done in the *marumage* style with a new blue band. She had been especially pleased by the hairdresser's compliments.

I immediately questioned her, "What happened, Mother?" But she made no reply. Scattered on the newspaper spread on the wooden kitchen floor were scissors, together with a shaping block, a chignon band, and a switch of false hair. I saw the paper cords for tying her hair cut in pieces and rolled into a ball. I pleaded, "Why have you taken down your hair? You just had it done yesterday."

As she towel-dried her hair, Mother turned to me and said, "I will no longer wear a *marumage*." "Why? Why?" I pressed her. Turning her face from me, she murmured, as if talking to herself, "Because its role is over," and she went to the porch. I did not understand what she meant by "its role is over," but somehow I felt I should question no further.

By lunchtime, she had done her hair herself in the *obako** style. My father, who by that time had risen and come down from the upstairs room, looked at her steadily and sullenly. In the kitchen Mother silently prepared his food.

Never since that time did my mother wear her hair in the *marumage* style.

Tanka-bai: *A Crude Language Sale*

 It might have been during the Bon Festival season of my third year in primary school that my grandmother came to stay with us at our home in Asakusa. We called her our "country grandma" because she was then living with my uncle's family in rural Takasaki. In her youth, however, Grandma had served as a woman-in-waiting in the Edo Castle where she had, as we heard, a romantic liaison and eloped with a young warrior during the confusing times of the Meiji Restoration. In spite of her age, she was still fair-skinned, tall and straight, and beautiful. She usually wore a *juban* [an undergarment] whose decorative white neckband showed at the edge of her *hitoe* [an unlined kimono] and a neat one-piece *obi* [sash] of black satin. Her exquisite *obako** hairdo was similar to the *katahazushi* style worn by the women-in-waiting of the Edo period. I admired this quiet and gentle grandma very much, but her extremely slow and graceful speech sometimes upset me. She spoke three times slower than I, a fast talker.

After dinner on the second day of her visit, she whispered to me, "O-Tei-chan, how about our going to the market at the temple and buying some 'panama' [bananas]." The first night of her visit, in the precincts of the Asakusa Kannon, she had seen a bargain on bananas. She was so enchanted by the vendor's spiel that she kept laughing, more like a titter, covering her small mouth with her right hand. Even to me as a child, the banana vendor's chatter was lively and refreshing, as was his appearance. With wisps of white hair on each side of his head, he looked nearly sixty. He wore a shirt of coarse cotton cloth, "pants" (more like the undergarments men wore then), and a *hara-maki* [a sash of coarse woolen cloth] to warm his belly. His lean face was deeply creased, and his narrow eyes looked sharp.

On a collapsible table with the top as large as a sliding shutter, he piled bunches of bananas and priced them one after another. As he hawked his wares, the vendor slapped the table for emphasis with something that looked like a yardstick, which he held in his right hand. It may have been a seamstress's ruler, tightly wound by a narrow strip of white bleached cotton and stained at the spot where he held it.

His patter and delivery were a real show: "Look! Look right here! What a great bunch, this is. Am I not right? All the way from Taiwan, across the sea, and look, no bruises. Look at the size. And the color—a beautiful yellow. See the sheen? They don't come any better than this. Open your eyes and look!" Then he slapped the table with his stick.

"Say there, little lady, that's right, Beautiful, you! I said, 'Open your eyes,' not your pretty mouth," he said to an attractive young woman who stood with her mouth agape at his antics. "Open your mouth like that, and you'll dribble all over yourself. Then where will all your good looks be?" Then he returned to his banter.

"Now, let's see," he continued as he held up the bunch again and paused for a moment. "I'd like to charge one yen and fifty *sen** for this beautiful bunch. But tonight is special. I'm here at the very merciful Kannon's temple. Out of respect for Him, I'll show mercy too." Then, with great flare, he said decisively, "I'll take the leap!" Then he slapped his stick on the table, and said, "One yen and twenty *sen*! That's my best price. You can't complain about that, can you?"

When no one responded, he stared at people in the crowd and said, "What's wrong? Are you sick or something? Are you all broke? All of you?" Then he pointed his stick at a well-dressed man standing at some distance from the stand and said, "Say there, that's right, you. You look like an educated man, a real gentleman. You must realize how nutritious these bananas are—and how inexpensive, too. What do you say?"

When the man in the crowd said nothing, the vendor said, "I know. I know! You're going to tell me you have no money. Well, isn't that too bad! If you have no money with all your education, then our world really is in bad shape, a dark day for us all." Then he stared at the man more intently and said, "Come to think of it, you do look kind of thin, not well-fed at all." Then he addressed the crowd again: "Here we have a case of malnutrition! Well, if we want to see this gentleman get well nourished and become a fine government official and save this Japan, I'll do my part. I'll knock off a little more." Slap! "One yen—my final price!" Then with a thud he threw the bunch on the table. As he continued, the vendor occasionally swore indiscriminately at one of the spectators as he highlighted his words by slapping the table with the stick: "May the devil take me! Let me take the mortal jump and knock it down to fifty *sen*."

The moment a customer who was familiar with the market price of bananas was certain he had heard the lowest possible price, he immediately shouted, "You've got a deal!" Then, the vendor would respond, "Take it, you thief!" and skillfully wrap the bananas in newspaper. As he handed over the package, his tone would change and he would say cheerfully, "Here you are. Thank you, sir." With a broad grin on his face, he would take up another bunch and begin again: "W-e-l-l, look here! This bunch is even more handsome than the one before."

This kind of marketing, in which the vendor's banter and actions, as well as his occasional crude language, are as important as the wares he is selling, is called a *tanka-bai* [a crude language sale]. The people of Asakusa enjoyed these immensely. They were much more fun than an ordinary play.

So when we went to buy "panamas," Grandma and I left home in high spirits, and she exclaimed, "Tonight I'll be the one to say 'You've got a deal'!" As we stood before the vendor's stall, Grandma grasped her purse tightly in front of her and stared straight ahead intently waiting for her chance. But she was unable to catch the right moment to shout her piece. Just as the vendor began the most entertaining part of his pitch, that is, when the price was still high, one yen and twenty *sen,* Grandma quietly stepped forward and said in her soft, studied speech, "Please allow me to buy that bunch of 'panamas.' Would you please be so kind as to sell it to me?"—all the time speaking in her usual maddeningly slow tempo. The moment Grandma had begun, I tried to stop her but it was too late. The vendor stood frozen, his stick held high. He was staggered, and he tottered. Then, he scowled at us with his sharp eyes and quickly wrapped the bunch of bananas and, without a word, handed it to Grandma. As he took her money, he looked the other way and jammed a Golden Bat cigarette in his mouth. His sullen profile reminded me of an actor who had struck a pose on the *hanamichi* [the elevated passage to the stage] and was about to deliver a powerful soliloquy when, suddenly, a voice from the gallery begins to cheer before a line has been uttered.

With her bunch of bananas under her arm, Grandma looked embarrassed and just stood there until I pulled her by the sleeve and we left. Her performance must have chilled the crowd, for as we left, I noticed that they, too, were leaving one by one.

The Yukata*, the Casual Kimono of Summer*

The other day, driving home from work, I glanced at a girl in a *yukata**, a summer kimono. Young girls today don't want to wear regular kimonos, saying they feel restrained by the number of cords. But in summer they do want to wear a *yukata*, which is much lighter and less restrictive. The girl I saw wore a *yukata* with a pattern that suited her well, large dragonflies arranged on a white background. Her solid yellow *obi* [sash], half the normal width, accentuated the effect. However, a pink decorative neckpiece showed at the edge of her *yukata*; this bothered me a little. Both men and women wear a *yukata* next to the skin. So wearing a *juban* [undergarment] under a *yukata* would be in as poor taste as putting a lining on lace; it would detract from its beauty and should be avoided. But if a woman feels she must wear an undergarment for modesty, an undershirt of bleached cotton, at most, is permissible—one that clings to the skin tightly and has no neckpiece. For similar reasons, neither white *tabi** socks nor *zori* sandals would be suitable with a *yukata*, while bare feet in *geta* [wooden clogs], a combination which looks cool and refreshing to the eye, would be quite appropriate. Because the girl I saw chose an attractive pattern and had a good figure, I regretted the way she wore her *yukata* all the more.

In former years, to enjoy the cool of evening men also wore *yukata* of their choice, as if competing with each other. Their wives or mothers could make *yukata* of a striped, checked, or octagonal pattern in one night. My father was particularly fond of his "towel *yukata*," which my mother sewed together from thirteen stylish towels of different patterns. When she finished it, Father was as pleased as a child. After a quick tub-bath in the backyard, he put on his new *yukata*, and off he went. To this day, I still recall his tall, swaggering figure retreating down the street.

About this time, Mother taught me the phrase "seven, five, three—and five *bu* more." As she told me, the knack for making a stylish man's *yukata* is to tailor the cloth in a much narrower width than for an ordinary kimono; seven *sun* [1.193 inches] for the back half, either right or left, five *sun* for the front half, and three *sun* for a gusset. "Five *bu* more"[one-tenth of a *sun*] means an additional five *bu,* at most, for a rather stout man. The phrase is easy to say, so I quickly learned it. I recall one time sitting face to face with Mother in the living room, which we had rearranged for summer. I spread out new cotton cloth for a *yukata* and cut it. The crisp sounds of the scissors going through the cloth is still fresh in my mind. I think this was one of my most pleasant moments of those days.

Today, I see young men wearing jackets next to the skin with gold chains as thin as thread dangling on their chests. A similar dandyism occurred in former days among the men walking the streets in their *yukata.* When passing such a man, young girls of Shitamachi, used to glance back and whisper to one another, "He's handsome, isn't he!"

The Hozuki[+] *Fair*

 The Hozuki Fair of Asakusa is held on July 9 and 10. In the precincts of the Senso-ji temple, booths are built overnight close to one another, and in each, pots of ground-cherries in bamboo baskets are beautifully displayed, every plant

---

[+]The *hozuki,* or "ground-cherry plant," is a member of the nightshade family and produces a fruit resembling a small tomato or cherry enclosed in a paper-thin calyx, and grows to a height of two feet. Children make whistles from the skin of the fruit and use them as toys.

having lavish clusters of red and green berries. Some booths sold ground-cherry dolls made from particularly large, red, ripe berries and clad in dresses of ornate *chiyogami* [a paper with colorful figures]. Imitations of the *hozuki*, called *naginata hozuki* and *uni hozuki*, were also available. They were so named because they were not ground-cherry skins but the egg cases of shellfish and thus tasted salty [*naginata* describes the blade-like shape of one type of sea *hozuki*, and *uni* is the general term for sea *hozuki*]. Here and there, between the ground-cherry stalls, were those that sold cotton candy, rice flour pastry, and *ame-zaiku* [figures made from a sweetened wheat mixture]—the usual scene at a fair.

People who pay homage to Kannon on the days of the fair are said to receive divine favors worth 46,000 days of pilgrimage. Therefore, the two days of the fair are also called the "forty-six thousand days." Many people come from distant places, and the precincts are crowded all day. After dinner, neighborhood residents, men, women, and children, stroll with round fans in hand, wearing *geta* and well-starched *yukata*, looking at the ground-cherries—a pleasant summer evening pastime.

I wonder how old I was, maybe less than ten, when my father, who was in an unusually good mood, took me to this fair. I had taken a tub-bath and Mother had patted my neck with plenty of powder to prevent prickly heat. I was happy and cheerfully followed my father. As we walked, we passed lightly powdered women whose appearance was neat and clean. They were blowing into the ground-cherry skins and making the usual squeaking sounds. On seeing their acquaintances, they smiled at each other and exchanged a few words.

My father bought me a small *naginata hozuki,* and when I stopped, absorbed in trying to produce the squeaking sound, my father patted me on the head and said, "Say, did you see the woman we passed? Isn't she attractive?" I was dumbfounded, but he continued, "I mean the woman who just spoke to me, that fair-skinned one with a *marumage* hairstyle." I quickly turned back and craned my neck to look. I glimpsed an attractive woman, who once again greeted my father by tilting her head. Grinning and stooping over to me, he whispered, "She . . . she used to be my woman. Though now she's married to another man." He said the name of a well-known storyteller, a name with which I was familiar although I was just a child.

I was stunned as I looked up at Father. He just winked triumphantly and walked on briskly. Pushing my way through the crowd, I tried not to lose sight of his slim figure. Then a sudden sadness seized me. I recalled that well-dressed women were always hovering about him. He talked about them as though flirtations were normal behavior—even to me, his young daughter. He seemed to regard them as medals of which he was quite proud. Mother always pretended not to hear Father's boastful and, in a way, innocent talk.

For the remainder of the fair, my heart ached for Mother in spite of the big pot of ground-cherries Father had bought me. When we arrived home, Mother noticed how despondent I seemed and said, "You must have caught a summer cold." She felt my forehead and said, "You have no fever, but you've had a busy day.

Perhaps you should go to bed early tonight." Without a word, I crawled into bed.

I never told Mother about what had happened that day.

Obon-sama†

At dawn, about five o'clock, on July 13, the Kusa-ichi Fair began in the area stretching from the Kaminari Mon [the thunder gate] of the Senso-ji temple to the corner of Tawara- machi—the Hirokoji intersection—an area several blocks westward from the gate. The fair occurred on the first day of the Bon Festival and provided booths where people could buy floral offerings and other essentials for the festival. Mother used to take me to the fair to buy ceremonial items to honor the spirits of our ancestors—an unglazed earthen vessel, a mat made of rush, and a shelf.

As we prepared for the festivals, I recall Mother often saying, "Today, the souls of our ancestors are coming home. We have to treat them with all the respect they deserve, don't we?" We placed the shelf before the family altar and spread the mat over it. There, we arranged early cucumbers, eggplants, and fruit. Mother used to

---

†During the Bon* Festival, tradition holds that the souls of ancestors return to their worldly homes. *O* and *Sama* are honorific, a prefix and suffix, respectively.

say, "This is the feast for the Obon-sama who have come after such a long walk from the other world." Toward evening, we made a sacred fire of wood chips in the earthen vessel, the *kawarake,* and placed it outside our door to light a welcoming path for the spirits.

Once, in a playful mood, I asked, "Mother, if all the families make similar fires, maybe our ancestors will go to another house by mistake." I pouted as if I were annoyed at our family being so superstitious. Mother answered in her typically generous way, "Don't worry, O-Tei. If our ancestors go to another house, others who are lost will come to us. Wherever they go, the families will treat them to a feast. It's a mutual arrangement."

Then I asked more seriously, "Mother, who were our ancestors?"

Mother paused thoughtfully and began "Well . . ."

Becoming more animated, I interrupted and asked, "Is it true that, until my grandparents' generation, Father's family ran a large wine shop and had so many warehouses that they had to be labeled alphabetically?"

Mother smiled and said, "I don't know about that. As you know, I married into that side of the family." Then, as she often did, she offered a maxim to place the issue in proper perspective: "They say, 'Things lost look large.'"

Not content with her answer, I pursued the matter further: "But Father's sister who lives on Umamichi Street said the family had been very wealthy."

Mother laughed and said, "How many gold teakettles our ancestors had is none of our business." Then she shrugged her shoulders and said, "It doesn't matter who our ancestors were. What matters is that, because of them, you and I now exist. Whoever they were, let's offer them a feast when they return for the Bon season."

At dinner that night, Mother did the best she could with the simple food available and prepared a meal consisting of vegetable dishes. But she placed a special plate of *sashimi* [raw fish served with condiments] on the table before Father's seat. Father, relishing Mother's offering, glanced at the Bon lantern hanging under the eaves, said "After all I am a living Buddha for this family. I deserve to be treated with reverence!"

Come to think of it, Father never spoke about our ancestors.

The Ryogoku Fireworks

 When the rainy season is over in mid-July, the houses in the narrow lanes of Asakusa are already hot and stuffy. After dinner, men go outside with fan in hand. Under the eaves of each house is a long wooden or bamboo bench which young men straddle as they play *shogi* [Japanese chess]. Sitting on a bench with one knee raised or with both legs crossed, men engage in animated conversations. When the dishes are done, wives come out, with their sleeves down and their kimonos opened a little at the neck to cool off. Frequently, one would look up at the sky and say,

"What a windless evening this is!" Children take tub-baths in the small gardens, and their mothers dab plenty of powder on their necks to prevent prickly heat. After they put on newly washed *yukata,* they sit on benches and look around at what is going on at other benches, bobbing about like kites.

Then a boy yells, "Look, everybody! I have some fireworks!" Immediately, all the children gather around him. A boy shouts, "Let me do it!" Next, a girl pleads, "It's my turn. Let me hold it!" They scurry about gleefully, shouting noisily, hoping to get a chance to play with some fireworks.

A *nezumi hanabi* [literally, a "mouse firework," which spins in circles on the ground] emits sparks and smoke and makes swishing sounds as it twirls. A sparkler spouts bright sparks in five different colors. Girls, sitting at the edges of a bench, assume a slightly affected pose and hold burning joss sticks at arm's length in front of them, creating cascades of sparks resembling flowers. They trade boasts such as, "My pine leaves are bigger and prettier than yours" or "Look at the chrysanthemum!" They compete to see whose joss stick lasts longest before it burns out, its dying ember dropping to the ground. Even men join them with a family-size box of matches and ask for joss sticks of their own.

One of the biggest displays occurred on July 21 each year, the fireworks at Ryogoku. Children dreamed of the large bursts of fireworks in the sky, like flowers momentarily opening high above them. Because the buildings were so close on the back streets of Asakusa, these fireworks were not visible, even though people craned their necks from the elevated platforms used for drying clothes. Nevertheless, whenever they heard the boom of a sky rocket, the children shouted in unison "Tamaya-a-a!" or "Kagiya-a-a!"[+]

Only once did we pester Father enough so that he agreed to take us on a boat ride to see the fireworks. My younger brother Tokunosuke and I were so happy that we told all our friends in the neighborhood of our plan: "We're going to see the Ryogoku Fireworks tonight! We're going on a boat ride down the Sumida River tonight." As I remember, it was a boat ride, all right, but the barge was so crowed that we didn't even have elbow-room. To make matters worse, a belligerent drunk seated next to me was very annoying. Somehow I also got the sleeves of my *yukata* wet and was on the verge of tears.

Still, seeing the fireworks from such a close vantage point was breathtaking; they were enormous and spectacular. One display called the "Niagara" ignited quickly, one section after another, creating a raging waterfall of falling sparks! I still recall Father and Tokunosuke's silhouettes backlit against the darkness.

◆　◆　◆

In the summer of the following year, my brother and I did not ask Father to take us to see the Ryogoku Fireworks again. We had heard some adults say that we could see them from platforms some restaurants had built specifically for viewing the fireworks. One person added, "If you really want to enjoy the fireworks, you must see them from a covered boat." Even as children,

---

[+]Tamaya and Kagiya are firms that have manufactured fireworks since the Edo Period.

we knew for sure that our family could not afford such extravagance. My brother said with some disdain, "Seeing the Ryogoku Fireworks is fun, but once is enough. Let's have our own fireworks with plenty of *nezumi hanabi* and sparklers. I'll buy you a ton of joss sticks, Sis. We'll have the Asakusa Fireworks!"

Despite his bravado, my brother and I still looked to the sky on the day of the fireworks and shouted somewhat wistfully, "Tam-ma-ya-a-a!" "Ka-gi-ya-a-a!"

Yabuiri: The Holiday for Apprentices

 In my youth, a common saying was, "The 'Lid of the Cauldron of Hell' is lifted on July 15 and 16." These are the second Yabuiri days, or the holiday for apprentices [An earlier Yabuiri holiday was observed in January].

From early morning, the Asakusa Park⁺ was crowded with apprenticed boys clad in striped livery, stiff sashes, and sporty caps; pretty servant girls with their hair drawn back into buns held in place by red combs; young men with their hair parted on the side and plastered down with pomade; and girls wearing their hair in the gingko-leaf style. They came not only from the city but also from the surrounding countryside.

⁺The Meiji government designated the precincts around Senso-ji temple as a park in 1883, a classification that remained until 1947 when the land was returned to the temple.

Leisurely glancing into shops of the Nakamise on the way to the temple, stopping to worship at the Kannon temple, and strolling around the Gourd Pond, young people came to Rokku for the main attraction for the day. There, a rich variety of amusements awaited them—movies; theatrical performances; an acrobatic show; a *gidayū* ballad drama [storytelling accompanied by music of the *shamisen*]; a *yasukibushi* recitation [folk songs originating from an area on the coast of the Sea of Japan]; an opera; a sword dance; roller skating. For a reasonable sum of money, young people could enjoy themselves to their hearts' content.

Ken-chan, an apprentice in a liquor store in my neighborhood, was mischievous and cheerful. However severely his fastidious master scolded him, Ken-chan seemed unconcerned, as if nothing had happened. He said he was an avid admirer of Matsunosuke Onoe, alias "Mat-chan the Eyeballs" [a well-known Nikkatsu movie actor, nicknamed for his ability to roll his eyes]. On the long-awaited day of Yabuiri, Ken-chan rushed straight to the Fuji Theater in Rokku and spent the day watching movies. He said, "To tell the truth, I even watch 'the train movie' at Lunar Park." The "movie house" in the park was an old third-class railroad coach where the audience sat in seats that rocked from side to side and watched two rails running endlessly through fields, projected on the screen before them. With no other scenery, the movie was monotonous. But when he saw this movie, Ken-chan felt as if he were traveling home to see his mother in distant Akita. "I have myself a little cry," he said, sticking out his tongue a bit as if ashamed of his confession. The "train movie house" was always full at Yabuiri.

Before the Great Kanto Earthquake of 1923, the most enticing attraction in Rokku was the single ticket admitting customers to three theaters, an idea introduced by the head of Negishi Show Business. With this ticket, people could see a performance by Soganoya Gokuro's troupe at the Tokiwa Theater. As soon as that ended, they could see an opera by standing at the Kinryu-kan. During the intermission, ticket holders could run to the Tokyo Club next door and enjoy a western action film. The three buildings were connected by a second-floor corridor. As I recall, the ticket was ten *sen* for adults, five for children. A movie admission in those days was about seven *sen,* so this economical ticket was very popular among young people.

Around Gourd Pond, booths crowded together provided food, such as curried rice, boiled beef and rice, *oden* [a thick fish stew], and boiled and seasoned *adzuki* beans. Boiled eggs sold for three for five *sen,* bananas, so much per bunch. Pears were peeled by a gadget that rotated around the inserted fruit, then placed on ice to cool. All these sold quickly, as if they had wings. I often heard of the apprenticed boys' upset stomachs from overeating during the Yabuiri holiday, so I suppose eating at one booth after another must have been a real treat.

Older people who knew every inch of Asakusa and relished fine food might go as far as Daikokuya, near the Denpo-in temple, to eat a large bowl of rice topped with fried fish; they always left satisfied. Food in Asakusa restaurants was always plentiful and good, and people welcomed its low price.

Nowadays people on any job take a day off every

week, and the practice of Yabuiri seems to be disappearing. In Tokyo, many entertainment districts with which I am unfamiliar have sprung up. With the Great Kanto Earthquake and the air raids during the last war—with each disaster, Asakusa declined. But recently the five-storied pagoda has been rebuilt, and, little by little, Asakusa seems to be regaining its former prosperity.

The Wife of the Year of the Cat[+]

O-Suga-san was born in the Year of the Monkey, like me, but one twelve-year cycle before me. She was twenty-eight then. Casually combing up her thick hair at the hairline, she drew it back into a bun. She wore her plain kimono with the edge of one collar neatly upon the other at her thin breast. Her dark face was unpowdered, her large eyes downcast, and her shapely lips tightly compressed. Her appearance suggested that she was fighting misfortune. Mother's sympathy made her say in O-Suga-san's absence, "She missed her chance to marry; I suppose she must be lonely."

Ten-odd years before, her father died suddenly. He was a construction worker whose debaucheries broke his wife's heart. As if following him, her mother also soon died, leaving O-Suga-san and her brothers orphans.

[+]See *"junishi"* in the Glossary.

Though her neighbors thought O-Suga-san was strong-minded and clever, providing for her two brothers and herself was too much for a fifteen- or sixteen-year-old girl. My aunt, a sewing teacher in O-Suga-san's immediate neighborhood, advised her to learn sewing. So O-Suga-san became her pupil and did odd jobs for her neighbors in the daytime and sewed at night. In time, the elder of her two brothers served out his apprenticeship to a carpenter, and the younger one finished primary school and apprenticed himself to a plasterer.

When she was finally freed from working like mad and could breathe easily, O-Suga-san was already past marriageable age. She was at that time my aunt's right hand and occasionally brought her finished articles to my home. My mother, who was by nature too eager to involve herself in the affairs of others, thought O-Suga-san's appearance was equal to that of most other women and was anxious to find her a suitable husband. Father, who was pessimistic about the prospect, said, "Very difficult, I bet. Her age is a problem, for sure, but she particularly lacks sex appeal—that's more serious. She's always stiff and awkward. If you touch her, she will go 'clank, clank.'"

Father was right. O-Suga-san's everyday language was stiff and formal, and her tone was strong and without feminine charm. So the young men in town did not have much to say about her. She had often said firmly and plainly: "I have stopped thinking of marriage. Nobody will marry an old maid like me. I don't want to be a burden to my brothers, so I'll make my living by sewing."

One night at dinner, Mother stopped serving in mid-

step and turned to Father when he said that he had seen
O-Suga-san, of all people, at the Hozuki Fair, beaming
as she walked—very closely—with Nikichi-san, the carpenter. He added, "At first I thought I had mistaken her
for someone else, for she had done her hair in the
gingko-leaf style. When I said hello, she turned around,
blushed, and hid behind Nikichi. She is in love, that
prim girl. How do you explain that?"

A month before, Mother had introduced O-Suga-san
to Nikichi-san, who happened to be repairing our
kitchen. This young carpenter, who did occasional work
for us, did not talk much but was a good-natured, hardworking man. He had a round face like a chestnut and
small, kind eyes. His master treasured this apprentice.
O-Suga-san, who had happened to come to our house
on an errand for my aunt, chatted with him over tea on
the porch, rare behavior for her. Perhaps Nikichi-san's
age and trade, the same as her brother's, made it easy for
her to talk with him. Nikichi-san spoke of how he
learned his trade: the precise rules for placing a plane
and a saw; the first lesson in carpentry, that is, to put the
workplace in good order; and his master repeatedly
hammering these lessons into him. O-Suga-san listened
attentively. That day she went home with Nikichi-san's
order for a *yukata*.

Nikichi-san had lost his parents and brothers in the
Great Kanto Earthquake of 1923 and lived alone in a
rented room above a candy shop in Shoden-cho. A few
days later, he was very chatty with Mother: "My land-
lady said that yesterday O-Suga-san brought my new
yukata and cleaned up my room while I was out. I bet
she couldn't bear it—my room was so messy. So sweet of

her, wasn't it? Her age . . . I wonder, is she two or three years older than I?" Mother did not dare to say that O-Suga-san was twenty-eight in the old way of counting age and answered with a laugh, "I don't know. How old is she? I wonder." Nikichi-san, who was twenty-three, finished his work in our kitchen that day.

The evening following the Hozuki Fair, O-Suga-san came to our home and sat in the living room. Mother and I looked at each other, waiting for her to speak. "I want you to hear something," she said, shyly lowering her head and revealing her slender neck. Her hair was done in the ginko-leaf style, and her posture had such sweet charm that I understood why Father had not recognized her at first.

"Is it about Nikichi-san?" Mother said, urging her to speak. O-Suga-san finally said, "I want to marry him." Her faint voice disclosed a sweetness I had never known in her before.

"That's wonderful," Mother said. "He is a hard-working man with a steady character. If that's what you want, I'll do everything I can to help you."

O-Suga-san raised her face suddenly, stared at Mother and said, "Please, please, never tell Nikichi-san my real age if he asks you. Don't tell him I was born in the Year of the Monkey—twelve years before O-Tei-chan. I told him I was born in the Year of the Mouse, that I am only a year older than he. O-Tei-chan, you, too, don't ever tell him my age. Please, please!"

Overcome by her anxious tone, I only nodded. Mother said, "All right. I understand. But, you, born in the Year of the Mouse! That was the year of your brother's birth."

O-Suga-san sighed as she said, "Last night, when he asked me to marry him, I unwittingly said, 'I'm older than you. Can you accept that? I am a year older than you; I was born in the Year of the Mouse.' The moment I said it, I remembered that my brother was born in that year. At first, I thought I would be caught. But it's possible. My brother was born in January, and I in December. If we pretend that we were born at the opposite ends of the same year, the problem disappears." In that case, her younger brother was born before her. O-Suga-san was very distracted and not thinking clearly.

Mother tried to soothe her, saying, "Nikichi-san knows you are older than he, yet he says he loves you. You shouldn't worry so much about your age." But O-Suga-san, shaking her head, continued: "If he knows I am five years older than he, he will be disillusioned, I'm sure. I will be so ashamed. If he finds out, I'll kill myself," she said and broke into tears.

To make the story more believable, we finally decided to reduce her brother's age by two years and pretend that he was born in January of the Year of the Tiger. However, Mother remembered another problem and added, "Nikichi-san will find out when your marriage is registered at the ward office."

"I don't mind leaving our marriage unregistered," O-Suga-san said.

Mother shot back: "Then what are you going to do when your baby is born? It will be illegitimate. The poor thing!"

"So . . . I will not have a child," O-Suga-san said in her usual stiff tone, returning to her former self. Yet, she continued, "Please, please, dear lady, don't tell anybody, please." She clasped her hands, as if praying and then left. As a young girl, I observed in amazement this great change that had overtaken O-Suga-san.

About ten days later, Nikichi-san came to our home. He apologized for being a little late in telling us, but he announced that he was going to marry O-Suga-chan. Because they both had few family members and their new home would be humble, they intended to have a simple wedding ceremony at his master's home. They would be honored to have our family attend. Nikichi-san's invitation was polite. But Nikichi-san's next remark upset mother: "I intend to register our marriage duly before the ceremony."

Mother stammered, "But . . . that won't . . ."

Quickly noticing Mother's confusion, Nikichi-san tilted his head to the side and shrugged mischievously and said, "I don't mind O-Suga-san's age. I have no education, and I like the kind of wife she will be, a woman older than I and of steady character. She was incoherently saying this and that about the Year of the Mouse and the Year of the Monkey. So I had a good talk with her last night and proposed to call her a wife of the Year of the Cat."[+]

That night, when Mother praised Nikichi-san's mature character for his age, Father remarked, stroking his chin knowingly, "That's an example of a bright woman and a dull man making a good match."

✦ ✦ ✦

That autumn, O-Suga-san visited Mother. O-Suga-

[+]There is no Year of the Cat in the *junishi* cycle of twelve years.

san was beautiful—a young wife wearing her hair in the *marumage* style with a pink chignon band. She happily told of having the sure signs of pregnancy. Then she said, "I am five years older than Nikichi-san by the traditional way of counting age, but the fact is I was born at the end of December and he on January 10, so the real difference in our age is four years and fifteen days."

O-Suga-san, beaming with joy to the point that she was hardly herself, raised her hand to her laughing mouth. On her third finger, I saw . . . a shining ring.

A White Mosquito Net

 In former days, Asakusa had many ditches and, consequently, many mosquitoes. Toward evening, countless mosquitoes began to swarm. With their paths entwining and weaving together, their wings produced a hum, and finally the swarm formed a column. From the time I was in the third grade of primary school, it was my daily chore to hang up, take down, and stow away the mosquito net.

For a child, the hemp net for a six-mat room [about 6 x 9 feet] was very heavy. The net was dark green with a red edge with metallic rings at the four corners and the two midpoints of its length. To hang the net, I stood on tiptoe on a stool to reach the hooks for the rings on the lintels. It seemed that every day my mischievous younger brother tickled the soles of my feet, and we got into a fight.

A greater nuisance than hanging the net was taking it down and folding it. I was a small girl and pulled one part of the net over another, struggling to fold it neatly. I usually crumpled the whole thing into a ball and thrust it into the closet. Then, of course, Mother scolded me. "How I hate a mosquito net!" I thought to myself. However, I rather liked sleeping under it.

The net covered almost the entire room. At night, when I softly shook the bottom, crouched, and slipped in, the odor of hemp greeted me. Later, sweating profusely, I awoke and glanced at Mother sewing outside the net. Her profile was then very beautiful. She was ladylike and looked like an unfortunate empress. And I, secretly watching her, was a loving princess, concerned for her mother. The story I had read during the day and the reality before my face entwined in my mind and somehow filled me with a bittersweet sense of rapture, leading me to sleep again. That mosquito net enabled a little girl to enjoy a whole range of dreams.

The Miyato Theater used a white mosquito net with pictures of autumn grasses at the bottom for the staging of *The Minowa Double Suicide*. At that time, I went to the theater every day to attend to my younger brother, who was a child actor. The play recounted the tragic love between a direct vassal of the Shogun with a fief yielding 5,000 *koku** of rice and a woman of the entertainment quarters. The last scene was at the home of his childhood nurse at Minowa. A lotus pond was stage right. Sitting on the open porch of a house stage left was Ayagimi the courtesan, who was cooling off. What caused me to stare in wonder was a beautiful white mosquito net behind her, one corner hanging loose, its upper edge a sky blue. Ayagimi sang this song:

> Which shall I take,
> You or five thousand *koku*?
> Let my fief be taken away,
> And I'll sleep with you.

The lyrics were incomprehensible to me. But I thought, "When I grow up I'd like to sleep under a beautiful mosquito net like that."

Strange things remain in a girl's memory.

Fingers

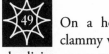 On a hot day, so hot my forehead was clammy with perspiration, the electric fan in the living room was rotating slowly. I was reading a newspaper, both of my hands pressing it down on the table. My husband, who sat across from me and was turning the pages of a book, murmured, "The skin on your knuckles seems so swollen!" Hearing his words, I looked at my hands and then said, "How true!" The knuckles of both hands were all raised, thick, and ugly. The scar from a burn I had suffered a few days before

from a splash of hot tempura oil on top of my left index and middle fingers was still red. On my right thumb was a cut, resulting from mishandling a can opener the day before. Feeling ashamed, I put my hands under the table, hoping my husband would not notice. But his eyes had already returned to his book.

✦ ✦ ✦

My elder brother Tomokazu was in the fifth or sixth grade, so I think I was about ten. The day was cold, with light snow falling. Three of us—my brother, his class-mate Koichi Yoshikawa, and I—were in the living room of our house in Asakusa. We were warming our hands, numb with cold, over a fire in the china brazier. Yoshikawa-san, heir to a branch temple of the Senso-ji, was my brother's close friend. They were both quiet boys, and whenever a bully taunted them with remarks such as "Look! An actor and a priest are playing together," they suffered their humiliation without talk-ing back.

I wonder what we three were talking about that day. My brother, looking at Yoshikawa-san's hands extended over the fire, suddenly commented, "Why, you have handsome fingers." I had been aware of that for some time. Yoshikawa-san's fingers were slender and fair. His fingernails had been pared short and, that day in partic-ular, shone as beautifully as a pink *sakura* shell.

"Well, my father says priests must keep themselves tidy because people look up to them. Yesterday I had my fingers polished with *tokusa* [the stalk of a variety of fern used for scouring]."

"Indeed!" my brother said. "Shall I polish my fingers with *tokusa*, too?"

Yoshikawa-san responded, "You already have nice-looking fingers. You play female roles. It's only natural, isn't it?" My brother's slender hands placed alongside Yoshikawa-san's were bluish, almost transparent rather than fair, perhaps because almost every day, he painted powder on them for the stage and later removed it.

"Show me your hands, Tei-bo," my brother demanded. And he quickly caught my hands which I was about to hide behind the brazier. "What's this?" he said. I was so ashamed. The tops of my index and middle fingers on both hands had dark-red scars from numerous scratches. My skin was thin and delicate, and I used a washboard poorly. In order to get the soles of *tabi* socks clean, I rubbed them vigorously against the rough washboard and often scratched the upper sides of my fingers. Mother had applied an ointment to them that very morning. She chided; "How helpless you are! If you washed a tubful of laundry, your fingers would be completely scraped away."

My brother released my hands and murmured softly, "This can't be helped, though. You are a girl. A girl has to do the washing. Poor thing!" Yoshikawa-san nodded sympathetically.

Fifty years have passed since then. These fingers have done plenty of work—and are still doing it, really, all kinds of tasks, such as spreading greasepaint and dabbing powder on my face, chopping radishes, and making *miso* soup. Finally they have become ugly things with raised knuckles. This can't be helped. For I am a "girl." For several years, now, I have stowed away the two or three rings I possess in special boxes.

I suppose they no longer fit these fingers.

Father's Change to Western Clothes

In my childhood, most men in the neighborhood dressed in kimonos. Only schoolteachers wore Western clothes. Others, such as the haberdasher and the confectionary shop owner, wore a kimono stylishly. My father looked particularly dapper in a kimono. In those days, Mother made him a stylish *tenugui yukata* out of Japanese cotton towels, which actors and geisha gave away as souvenirs. Father wore the *yukata* casually when he went to the public bath. Watching his retreating figure, I thought he looked fashionable, mere child that I was.

Because my father was the lord of the house, my mother did everything for him. But he did not allow her to touch his wardrobe. When he was preparing to go out, Father went to his chest of drawers and, one at a time, chose a kimono for that day and other articles of clothing. With his long fingers, Father carefully held the kimono by the neckband of fine linen, perhaps one of his favorites, the one with a splashed pattern to suggest a swarm of mosquitoes. He swirled the kimono around in the air and softly slipped it onto his shoulders. Placing the left side of the kimono across his chest on top of the right side, then securing the front with his left hand, Father quickly wound the stiff Hakata sash around his waist. The way he did it all was marvelously clever. Then he neatly folded the kimono he had taken off and put it away.

My father had been indentured to a pawnbroker for ten years from the age of twelve because my grand-

father's intemperance ruined the family's wholesale *saké**
business. During that time, he was taught how to han-
dle kimonos properly. When it was time for his master
to set him up as a pawnbroker, Father suddenly asserted
that he aspired to be an actor and caused his master and
my grandmother much anguish. His action was quite
understandable: My father was tall and handsome like
the famous actor Uzaemon the Fifteenth. However,
Father's dream did not come true. Instead he was briefly
a playwright and later a member of the production staff
of a Kabuki troupe.

When he stood at the left end of the stage, clapping
wooden clappers, his body half hidden by the curtain,
Father usually wore a kimono and no *hakama** [a formal
outer garment]. At these times, he was very much a
topic of conversation among the wives and young girls
of Shitamachi. "My, he is good-looking, isn't he?" they
said. Every time our neighbor the draper had kimonos
in new patterns, he set one aside for Father and asked
him to wear it. It was as if he were a fashion model for
kimonos. Father, who was always jovial, took every
occasion to brag about his appearance to me: "Women
used to wait for me at the stage door. I was much more
popular than any second-rate actor!"

✦ ✦ ✦

It was summer, and Father was over fifty. A few days
before he was to leave for Manchuria with his troupe on
a tour, he stood proudly before Mother and me, wearing
a brand-new Western suit. He said, "Just take a look. I
don't look bad, do I?" The dark-blue alpaca coat had a
stand-up collar. Father, who had a long torso, stood with

his sloping shoulders raised and his slender legs braced. Above his oval face, a stiff straw hat sat awkwardly. I wondered in astonishment, "Where is the sense of style he has when wearing a kimono?" In spite of myself, I would have said, "Stop, Father. No Western clothes, please!" But the sight of Mother, standing beside him nodding and smiling, kept me from saying so.

That night, when I was in bed, Mother whispered to me, "He is definitely less attractive in those clothes. But he's happy with his new coat. Why disillusion him? We should take his age into consideration. Besides, on a long trip Western clothes are more convenient and allow easy movement. Just wait and see. We know he is a good dresser. In time he will learn to wear Western clothes well."

Father continued going to work in Western clothes from then on, but he never learned to wear them well. About this time, his trysts with women became less frequent and eventually stopped completely.

Perhaps it was Mother who advised Father to wear Western clothes. This idea occurs to me lately, and I smile secretly.

No Crying

51 "A girl must not cry. She must be patient, very patient in everything," Mother taught me when I was about to shed tears. When I asked why a girl must not weep, she answered simply, "If you cry, you won't prepare meals on time."

The eighth year of Taisho [1919] was the year of a nationwide depression, and many banks closed their doors. The small savings that my parents had accumulated by cutting down on food and clothing was lost in a single night. Father crouched in the living room crying, but Mother was busy in the kitchen cooking. She was doing her best to encourage Father to eat some food. He had eaten nothing since morning.

Her eyes were brimming with tears. But she did not cry.

Pickles with Ochazuke*

 My mother was very fond of pickles. When savoring *ochazuke*⁺ with pickles—pickles made from eggplant with a luster of bright blue, from dark green cucumber, and from small turnips—Mother seemed to be the happiest woman in the world, completely satisfied.

As a lover of pickles, Mother was good at preparing them. She placed a one-*to* barrel [five U.S. gallons] in the storage area beneath the kitchen floor—in those days, most homes had this convenient space. Three times every day—in the morning, in the middle of the day, and in the evening—every time she put in vegetables to be pickled or took some out to be eaten, she mixed the contents of the barrel thoroughly from bottom to top. When she removed the lid, a fragrant aroma floated through the air. She always kept the barrel's sides wiped clean. While mixing the contents, she repeated some of her favorite phrases: "The *nukamiso* [the rice-bran paste and salt which causes the pickling] will get tired if I don't keep it stirred up." "We must let the *nukamiso* breathe in fresh air." "The *nukamiso* has a life of its own." These views certainly explained the care with which she treated the paste. She always spread a dry dishcloth on its surface, which she smoothed with her palm. This cloth, which absorbed moisture, was changed in the evening. Once a month, Mother roasted new rice bran, and after cooling it, added it to the paste.

⁺*Ochazuke* is simply a bowl of rice with tea poured over it.

This procedure seemed to be the secret of her pickling. She must have learned it by trial and error.

From time to time, she removed vegetables left too long at the bottom of the barrel, cut them into tiny pieces, washed them in water, and mixed them with the juice from squeezed ginger, soy sauce, and dried bonito shavings. We then ate the mixture on top of hot rice. Thanks to her, I acquired a taste for this delicate flavor.

Mother's fondness for pickles may run in my blood. Pickles have been my favorite food since I was young, and I always make crunching sounds when I eat them. Once a day, I thrust my arm above the elbow into the barrel and carefully mix the paste. When I tell young actresses about this, they look amazed, but I tend my barrel simply because I want to enjoy these delicious pickles. A large thermometer hangs near the movable floorboard of our kitchen storage area so I can pickle vegetables earlier on a cold day and later on a warm day.

When Mother taught me the precise way to pickle vegetables in order to eat them at such and such a time of the day, she often hummed a song I still recall:

> Eggplant is ripe for pickling
> And a girl is ripe for marriage. . . .

I am nearing her age now.

Colored Neckbands

 For the last ten or fifteen years women have worn only white replaceable neckbands, rather than colored ones, with their *naga-juban* [a long undergarment], whether they wear everyday clothes or their best dress clothes. When I appear in a television or theatrical play, I always choose a costume to fit my part beforehand. But unless I take the utmost care to remind the person in charge of costumes of my choice of accessories, it happens that I, the Shitamachi wife of the owner of an *odenya** [here, a small, inexpensive restaurant], have no other neckband than one as white as the whites of turned-up eyes. Then I become flustered.

In earlier days, women of Shitamachi wore a white neckband only on formal, ceremonious occasions. "Sometime later, I'll call on you wearing a white neckband" was an everyday phrase women used. It means "I'll pay you a *formal* call." In order to accentuate the bride at a wedding ceremony, we were told to refrain from wearing a kimono with a design at the bottom [that might attract attention]. For the proper attire at a relative's funeral, the women said, "We don't have money enough to own a garment only worn for mourning," so they made dark kimonos with fine, subdued patterns. This Shitamachi spirit may have kept alive that common form of greeting.

Purple, brown, or pale yellow bands showed at the neckline of everyday kimono. Young girls always wore neckbands without a pattern, in red, pink, and a variety of colors. Women of the geisha world sometimes wore tie-dyed neckbands. And when women wore two-layered kimonos as visiting wear, their neckbands were embroidered with plum, cherry, willow, and peonies, in threads of gold, silver, and other colors—embroidery that matched the kimonos.

Even now many of my friends in Asakusa wear colored neckbands without a pattern. Very often, to the curious amazement of young people, I wear deep purple and silver gray neckbands. Somehow, wearing a white neckband, I feel uneasy and, above everything else, tense. This is how an old convention affects me. Strange, I think. Even a faint stain on a white neckband bothers me, although I simply can't throw it away. For a Shitamachi woman—so particular about cleanliness and ill-at-ease unless she wipes clean the frame of her latticed front door to the point of thinning it—a colored neckband, which does not reveal a little soiling, feels more comfortable.

If only to a small degree, a colored neckband also conceals fine wrinkles on a woman's face. I have dyed to some other color white neckbands that I have worn a few times for formal wear or with a mourning dress. I think this is a good economical measure. These neckbands look stylish if worn properly, though I hardly recommend the practice for those whose primary concern is elegance.

A midsummer scene from long ago still comes back to me. One sultry day, when the fingertips, in a manner of speaking, almost oozed sweat, a woman seated in a box at the Miyato Theater gently fanned herself. From her demeanor, she seemed as refined as the wife of the owner of a large store. Her very figure was refreshing. Her hair was done in a rather tight *marumage* style, and she wore a kimono of fine white linen and a gray sash from Hakata.

What set off her figure was a linen neckband of dark blue.

The Platinum Koi⁺ Ring

 It was 1923, the twelfth year of Taisho. In spite of August's usual slump, the Miyato Theater was active with its successful summer production, *A Ghost Play: The Peony Lantern*. In the play, O-Tsuyu, the beautiful daughter of a samurai warrior serving the Shogun, having died of love for a young masterless samurai, visits her lover almost every night. She is led by her nurse holding a lantern on which a peony is painted. As she enters, the "clank-clank, clank-clank" of her clogs precedes her from the darkness of the stage. The audience held its breath at the eerie atmosphere of the scene and was moved by O-Tsuyu's pitiful and lovely woman's heart. So the summer play ran.

My older brother, Tomokazu, played O-Tsuyu, his first woman's role. Under the stage name of Kozuchi Sawamura, he enjoyed more popularity than expected

---

⁺*Koi* is a fish of the carp family, prized in Japan for its beauty.

and happily entered the greenroom every day. He was then in his nineteenth year by *kazoe*.*

One morning after the middle of the play's run, Mine-san the hairdresser dropped in on us on his way to work at the theater. He related that Sazanami, the young head courtesan at the Kadoebi, a brothel in Yoshiwara, came three times to see the play, accompanied by geisha from the house. Mine-san confided to us, "The object of Sanzanami-san's visits is your Kozuchi-san. Everybody says she is head over heels in love with him."

Boiling green soy beans in the kitchen, I heard Mine-san's whispers and felt blood rise to my cheeks, though his talk had nothing to do with me. Father, who looked forward to his son's future as a young actor of female roles, was happy to hear of Brother's popularity, but Mother listened as if under a dark cloud. Mine-san left, happy to have his share of the courtesan's tips when she came to the play.+

Toward the end of the month, four days before the close of the run, Brother stayed out overnight for the first time. He came home toward dawn. I was awakened by Father's shouts upstairs. Astonished, I was about to sit up in bed when Mother, by my side, stopped me softly and quietly went upstairs. After a while, she returned and said that Brother was not allowed to sleep under the mosquito net. She added that as he listened to Father, Brother sat obediently, his head lowered.

Before noon the next day, Brother came downstairs, looking pale from lack of sleep. He hurriedly ate break-

---

+Patrons gave money to theater workers as well as to the actors to show their approval.

fast and silently left for work with barely enough time to make it to the greenroom. I tried to read his thoughts by looking at his drooping face, but no clue was visible to a sixteen-year-old girl.

On the last day of the month, I came home a little after noon from an errand. Turning into our lane, I saw a sight that stopped me in my tracks. A young woman, a stranger, was standing before our lattice fence by the kitchen door. She looked like a peony blooming out of season in the strong midsummer sun. With a sky-blue parasol folded in her left hand and her right fingers inserted into her ample bosom, her full-figured body swayed impatiently, her head lowered. She wore her hair in the gingko-leaf style, and her kimono of Akashi silk crepe was in stripes of black and white. The way she wore her brown Hakata sash, a little lower than is usually done, looked amateurish, but what struck me was the dazzlingly bright scarlet silk crepe of her sash bustle.

Noticing that I was coming slowly toward her, the woman raised her head. Her thick brows, red lips, and exceptionally black, gaping eyes met mine. An aroma of powder arose from her white face. Her forehead was perspiring slightly at the hairline. This, I instantly knew, was the Sazanami-san I had heard about, but at that moment, I was speechless.

With short steps, a lean older woman came from our latticed door and whispered to the young woman, "He is out. They say he went to Hakone after the play last night." In spite of myself, I cast down my eyes. Brother was then sleeping in the upstairs room. I knew that a benefactor had invited him to Hakone the next evening.

Sazanami-san strode straight to me and said, "You are

his sister, aren't you? Please tell your brother I will wait tonight. If he can't come, I'll come for him again tomorrow." Her voice was low and sweet. She pulled a ring from her finger and put it in my right palm and squeezed my hand with both of hers. They were soft and cold. I stood there blankly without resisting.

"Let's go, quick," she said to her attendants. Turning up her nose, she pivoted and pattered away briskly in her black-lacquered clogs. She did not even look back. After she left, a faint fragrance of perfume hung in the air. I timidly opened my hand and saw a large heavy ring. A platinum *koi* two centimeters long was twisting itself in golden waves. The *koi*'s eyes were two shining diamonds.

When he heard my story while drinking tea in the living room, Brother said, "Just keep it. Don't worry about it." Then he suddenly went upstairs. Mother sighed, "How embarrassing! We must return it later." On the tea table, she wrapped the ring in a silk batting and stowed it deep in a cabinet drawer. That night, at Father's command, Brother suddenly went to Hakone.

✦ ✦ ✦

At noon the next day, September 1, the Great Kanto Earthquake occurred. Many lives were lost. Although our home burned to the ground, miraculously our lives were spared. Our family survived. Luckily Brother, in Hakone, was able to crawl out from the roof of the collapsed hotel and suffered only a minor injury. Three days later we learned that many Yoshiwara courtesans had died in the Gourd Pond of Rokku, Asakusa. What had become of Sazanami-san? I wondered.

Passing the night under the great gingko tree in the park and looking up at the starlit sky, I recalled the black pupils of Sazanami-san's eyes which absorbed me. My heart ached, but I could not bring myself to mention my anxiety. I knew no one in my family would want to hear the cause of my worry.

The platinum *koi* ring, stowed deep in the cabinet drawer that day, was destroyed in the fire and no trace of Gourd Pond remains in the park.

Nihyaku-Tōka

 "Oh, my," Mother sighed, "the calendar is right, after all!" It was *nihyaku-tōka*, the 210th day [approximately September 1] from the first day of spring [usually February 4]. In the afternoon, the wind began to roar, and a strong rain drenched our narrow open porch. On such days, the hearts of small children throbbed in anticipation of excitement—although they ducked their heads in fear. For children of Asakusa, whose daily lives on the back streets lacked adventure, heavy rains and strong winds were a welcome change.

Our house at Umamichi had no glass doors or windows. So if we pulled the sliding shutters tight, our house was quite dark. On stormy days, Mother removed a middle shutter and placed it on its side tightly between the adjacent shutters. She created this makeshift window, three feet high and six feet long, for us children when we had to stay inside the small rooms of our house. From this window, we stuck out our heads and saw a *yatsude** [evergreen] shrub and maple and fig trees bent under the heavy rain almost to the point of breaking. We enjoyed seeing our garden so much more active than usual.

I recall one *nihyaku-tōka* that seems so typical to me now. As often happened, the rain stopped momentarily, then it poured again, and the wind showed no sign of ceasing. As time passed, my bored brothers began sword fights, using Mother's rulers as weapons. They pulled open the cabinet drawers and formed a "staircase" suitable for them to climb. With a two-foot ruler in one hand, my big brother charged to the top of the cabinet, jumped with a thud to the *tatami* mat floor, and pretended he was in battle as he hummed a *shamisen* tune—*chan, chan, chan, chaka-chaka-chaka.* My little brother carelessly brandished a one-foot ruler right and left. As always, in a house with only two rooms, this play ended in no time with torn *fusuma** [sliding doors dividing rooms] and *shoji** [sliding paper screens] full of holes.

I was helping Mother unstitch old clothes and sew on patches and protested every time they made holes in the *shoji*. But Mother wasn't bothered. She laughed and said, "Don't worry, O-Tei. It's okay. They can't play outside today, so it can't be helped." Taking advantage of her leniency, my brothers ran wild. Then Mother spoke to me in a low voice: "Too many 'don'ts' to stop boys' mischief cause them to grow into fussy men." Perhaps she was so tolerant because she didn't think broken *fusuma* and *shoji* were worth complaining about. And our furniture wasn't so valuable that they could hurt it.

The next day, when the calm made the storm seem like a dream, the slender trees and plants in the garden bathed in the sun of late summer, as if a storm had never occurred. But on our *fusuma* and *shoji* unexpected flowers bloomed. Cut from white, red, and yellow wrapping paper were patches in the shape of plum and cherry flowers—the fruits of Mother's labor.

Matt-san the Niō *

 Matt-san's[+] *odenya** [a small, inexpensive restaurant specializing in *oden,* a form of Japanese stew] in Umamichi was nine feet wide and six feet deep and seated only two or three customers—more like a large street stall than an eatery. When we passed his shop, a tantalizing aroma greeted us. Customers heartily enjoyed the combination of ingredients, cooking and steaming in the large pot. Matt-san used good stock, and many housewives brought bowls and bought the food he prepared. In the summer a glass-bead curtain chimed in the wind, and Matt-san's shop sold shaved ice and *tokoroten* [a gelatinous summer favorite made from processed seaweed

---

[+]"Matt-san" is a colloquial pronunciation of Matsu-san. A Niō is the guardian god at a temple gate.

and served in strips with vinegar]. The gooey sweetness of shaved ice with boiled *adzuki* beans tasted especially good. Near his shop, at the bottom of ten stone steps was Matt-san's house on a small patch of low ground.

Before he started his *odenya*, Matt-san drove a *rik-isha** [a small, two-wheeled, manpowered taxi]. Women of the geisha quarters often sent him to our home to fetch Father. Because he was particular about the way he dressed, Father kept Matt-san waiting while he carefully changed clothes. When I was five or six years old, I enjoyed standing at our lattice door and looking at his polished *rikisha*. One day, he said to me, "Hey, Tei-bo. Like a ride? Let me give you one." Matt-san lifted me onto the seat and, bellowed, "*A-ra-arya-arya*. Make way for Tei-bo!" Then he gave me a brief tour of the neighborhood. Matt-san was tall like a Niō with square shoulders and thick arms like logs. Although a brawny man, his good-natured round eyes smiled beneath the deep wrinkles of his sunburned forehead.

When he was too old to pull a *rikisha*, Matt-san started his *odenya* on the advice of his wife, who had lived with him for forty years. Short and thin and much older looking than her husband, she had a gentle way of speaking and, because she was a good listener, everybody liked her. With a cord holding up her sleeves and neatly wearing an apron on her fragile frame, she was always busy preparing food for the shop.

Matt-san was very considerate of his wife, although his words didn't reflect it. If she tried to lift a heavy pail, he got angry and shouted, "I told you I would do it. Didn't you hear me, you pumpkinhead?" And, picking it up with one hand, he took it away instantly. A brash young man, seeing this behavior, made fun of him, saying, "A proverb says 'A fleet steed grown old runs slower than a jade,' so I see Matt-san the Niō grown old is under his wife's thumb." Matt-san just listened, grinning, pipe in mouth, and said, "She has suffered a lot from my ways. We are nearing the end of our lives, and I want her to take it easy now and have good memories of her life."

Matt-san said that drinking, gambling, and whoring would always be part of a man. Even if he tried, a man couldn't break these habits until the right time came. A true woman would endure it all with no complaints and remain faithful to her husband. He said the white hairs of such a wife would encourage a man to give up these three bad habits for good. Then he added, "What she has done for me all these years without ever complaining! I don't deserve it! A man can't help but give in to a faithful woman's heart. However, if she complains or argues, I'd kick her butt." What he said showed how self-centered men are, but, because I didn't want to be kicked by his giant foot, I listened to him without making a comment.

Being the kind of man he was, Matt-san was displeased when he learned that I had been admitted to a girls' high school. I was celebrating my admission by myself over the choicest *mitsumame* [a confection, particularly popular with young girls] when he said, "I am disappointed with you, Tei-bo. Why on earth are you going to high school? No good comes from a girl going beyond primary school. Can you imagine a girl bragging about her learning? Even a beautiful girl would ruin her appeal. Give up this idea! Make yourself better-looking, and find a good husband. A woman is happiest when loved as a wife. Her happiness depends on who her husband is." His talk gradually became more emotional, and he reasoned with me in a touching tone, finally almost in tears. His wife was nodding beside him. In spite of their sincere advice, I saw the couple less frequently after I began attending high school. One reason, though, was that I was busy with both schoolwork and a part-time job as a tutor.

✦ ✦ ✦

Two years later, on September 1, 1923, the Great Kanto Earthquake struck, and the Shitamachi area turned into a sea of flames. When autumn came, makeshift huts appeared here and there, but Matt-san and his wife never returned. Because he was a strong man, Matt-san must have put his wife on his back with ease, run from the fire to safety—somewhere—and there lived the remaining years of their lives in peace. This is what I wish to believe.

The Sap of the Sponge Gourd

 Every year, toward the end of the rainy season [early June to mid-July], Mother planted a sponge gourd beneath our kitchen window. Although it enjoyed only a few hours of sunshine daily, the plant always grew well.

On the night of the full moon in September, Mother cut the climbing plant about one and a half feet above the ground, bent the stem, and inserted it into the mouth of a one-*sho* [0.477 U.S. gallon] bottle, covering the mouth carefully with oiled paper. The sponge gourd, thus cut, was no longer able to bloom nor bear fruit but would continue sucking water from the ground as vigorously as ever. Drip, drip, drip, the sap filled half the bottle in a month.

Mother added a little boric acid to the sap, then boiled and filtered it through a cloth. This was Mother's skin lotion, which lasted her an entire year. She didn't use anything else. Perhaps the gourd lotion explained why, in her old age, Mother's skin was still in good condition in spite of her wrinkles.

Sponge gourds climbed bamboo fences all along the alleys of Asakusa.

The Tiger of Goo *[Saturn]*

 Some years after he turned fifty, Father stopped philandering for good. He had no choice—women were no longer attracted to him. The women he had dallied with were mostly from the geisha quarters. Madly infatuated with him, they competed for his attention and spent a great deal of money on him.

Father believed himself to be—and others concurred—much more handsome than the ordinary actor, and freely allowed himself to take whatever was offered. Being a ladies' man, he thought it natural for women to wait upon him. I recall hearing him say, "Why should a man spend money on a woman? It's a disgrace!" With neither money nor power, Father could boast only of his appeal to women. But, as he advanced in years and no more *rikisha* came to fetch him, his dalliances ended.

When he became more of a homebody, Father began to recognize Mother as a weightier presence. Although he retained extravagant and self-indulgent habits and remained lord of the household, he came to realize that, without Mother, his life would not run smoothly. Before this time, he had regarded Mother merely as a childbearing machine.

Mother proved herself a person of substance at the time of the Great Kanto Earthquake in 1923. She helped my brothers and me to escape to the woods of Ueno, handing us an iron kettle, pieces of dried bonito, and a tub of boiled rice as we fled. Father was paralyzed with terror when the house shook as if the end of this world had come, and Mother dragged him until they finally reached the precincts of the Senso-ji temple. In the firestorm that engulfed the area, only the temple avoided destruction and provided a refuge.

On the third day after the catastrophe, I returned to the still-smoldering ruins of my neighborhood, pouring water on my feet from time to time to alleviate the heat. I found my parents under the tall gingko tree beside the main building of the temple. Father's long nose, his pride, was scraped, and he looked pitiful and dejected. But Mother, who had dug in the ruins of a *miso* store and a butcher's shop nearby and found some burned *miso* and meat, was preparing a meal for Father.

Knowing her place, Mother always paid due respect to Father, but, when troublesome problems arose, she quickly settled them behind the scene. Glancing sideways at her, Father often said to me, "I can never get the best of your mother. She was born in the Year of the Tiger and *Goo* [Saturn]. And I was born in the Year of the Rabbit and *Shichiseki* [Venus]!" According to Father, the tiger of Goo is strong-spirited enough to devour its opponents, while the rabbit of *Shichiseki* is less exuberant and gentle-natured.

Father and Mother were not a devoted couple in their life together. Perhaps the stars they were born under were to blame. However, it seems to me, in the bottom of her heart, Mother loved Father. On the anniversary of Father's death (he died soon after the end of the Pacific War), Mother always offered his favorite dishes at the family altar: *tempura**, eel, and *sashimi**. She lamented, "In his last days, such luxuries were not available. I felt so sorry for him."

If Father had lived a little longer, Mother could have served him these delicacies. As Mother told me this, tears rolled down her cheeks—tears from the one who had never before shed tears, whatever the adversity.

The Tale of the
Manseian Noodle Shop

 Formerly, the area behind the Senso-ji temple in Asakusa was called Okuyama. When I was a child, a large *soba* [buckwheat noodles] shop called the Manseian was located there. Off the main street to the temple was a lane, and at the corner where it crossed another path, the Manseian's roofless gate bisected the fence, which was made of beautifully grained timber from an old ship. From this gate the restaurant's lovely garden was visible.

On the grounds that seemed as large as a full three-hundred *tsubo** [about a quarter of an acre] stood the main house with several stylish smaller buildings surrounding it. Here and there along the narrow gravel paths connecting these houses were large stone basins, always brimming with cool, clear water. Interspersed among shapely pines, maples, box trees, and *maki* [Chinese black pine] bloomed flowers of each season— plum, peach, camellia, peony, and wisteria. Almost every day a gardener wearing *kyahan* [cloth leggings extending from the knee to the ankle] tended them.

The tradition of this old shop was evident from the neat dress of the shop employees. Befitting a fine restaurant, the maids wore aprons and no face powder; their sleeves were pulled up and tied with cords, suggesting their brisk activity; and their hair was fixed in the gingko-leaf style. The restaurant was particularly known for its universally polite treatment of all guests. People of Asakusa used to say, "The Manseian is number one.

The way the proprietor trains his employees is far better than in other restaurants." They were proud of the Manseian, as if it were their own shop.

To the frequently asked question, "What is your most tasty dish?" the waiters were taught to reply immediately, "*Zaru-soba* [*soba* served on a bamboo tray] is the best." The Manseian's *zaru-soba* had no flakes of roasted *nori* [dried seaweed, pressed into paper-thin sheets] sprinkled on top. If guests wanted *nori*, waiters brought them a *nori* container, a cube of fine, handmade paper covering a wooden frame placed on a coal-filled receptacle the size of a tobacco tray [six to eight inches]. Inside was a sheet of crisp, dried Asakusa *nori*. The guests crushed the *nori* in their hands and sprinkled the tiny flakes over their noodles. The guests embraced this elegant way of serving.

I cannot say for certain, but I think in those days *zaru-soba* was five *sen* and the *nori* an additional two *sen*. A bowl of *tempura-soba* [buckwheat noodles topped with deep-fried fish] or *kamo-namban* [noodles with duck meat mixed with green onions] was popular. The Manseian's *nabeyaki* [boiled noodles served in the small pot in which it was prepared] was also highly regarded because of its unique blend of thirteen different ingredients. Yet the owner believed that the main draw of a *soba* shop should be the taste of its *zaru-soba*.

People flocked to the Manseian, relishing a tray of *soba* while enjoying the view of the spacious garden, so its rooms were always crowded. Every year visitors to the Kannon temple for the Hozuki Fair and the Hagoita* Fair dropped in at the Manseian. Many, entering by the gate near the Sanja-sama* shrine, walked through the garden, found all the seats taken, and left by the back gate on the main street. The cheerful waitresses would bow politely and call out to them, "Thank you for your patronage. I hope you enjoyed our humble offerings." Treated in such a friendly way, the guests left without complaint and often returned. Their accounts of the restaurant and its service increased the popularity of the shop even more.

On the Sanja Festival day, important men of the town, in *montsuki* [kimono bearing the family crest] and formal *hakama* [a skirt-like outer garment], gathered at the temporary altar set up in the garden for serving refreshing drinks. High-spirited leaders of various trade guilds relaxed together in groups of two and three. I still remember the picturesque spectacle of the scene.

✦ ✦ ✦

I was twelve or thirteen years old when I first saw the *okamisan** [proprietress] of the Manseian. Father, Tomokazu, and I passed the main house after having *soba* when the woman quietly rose behind the counter's lattice screen and our eyes met. She bowed slightly to us and retreated into the kitchen. Father said, "She is the *okamisan* everybody talks about. Isn't she a beauty? Her charm irresistible? Few actors can produce that romantic quality." Tomokazu, who played a girl's role at the Miyato Theater, added, "More than anything else, her figure is superb. It captures a man's heart." Father continued in this vein: "After all, she was a young geisha of rising fame in this area. She has the sensual appeal of the Edo style that she acquired in her childhood." Their conversation about her continued for some time.

The *okamisan,* O-Tome-san, appeared to be twenty-one or twenty-two. Her hair was done in the neat *maru-mage* style of a married woman, with side tresses and a simple chignon—a pink band holding it in place. Her vertically-striped cotton kimono had a black satin neck-band, under which showed the light blue *han-eri* [a replaceable neckpiece for her undergarment]. The hem of her kimono was raised a bit higher than usual for easy movement. With a lovely purple *obi* sash from Hakata [a place known for producing beautiful *obi* sashes], an apron, a cord tucking up her sleeves, and deep blue *tabi* socks, she was breathtakingly beautiful. Her lithe figure, oval face free from powder, and limpid eyes added to her tantalizing allure.

Listening to Father praise O-Tome-san's beauty, I recalled my aunt and mother speaking of her. My aunt, who earned her living by doing needlework in her home behind the Asakusa Primary School, had formerly lived near the Ohaguro Channel in Ryusenji-cho, Shitaya. The owner of a small candy store there had many children, so many, in fact, it reminded me of the saying on a child's "alphabet" card. In order to decrease the number of mouths to feed, they gave up the eight-year-old O-Tome-chan for adoption. When it was said that O-Tome-chan was to become the daughter of a man who owned the geisha* house called the "Kusanoya," my aunt pitied this innocent girl so much that she was unable to sleep the entire night, worrying about the hardships the child would experience.

As fate would have it, two or three years later, through someone's recommendations, my aunt, who had moved from Ryusenji to the neighborhood of the

Asakusa Primary School, began to take in sewing from the Kusanoya geisha house. In the meantime, O-Tome-chan from the candy shop had slipped from her mind. But my aunt soon learned that, contrary to her fears, O-Tome-chan had been treated well and had grown into a carefree, beautiful girl. My aunt was very much relieved, as if the girl were her relative.

In those days Asakusa had five first-rate restaurants called the "Five Houses"—the Daikin, the Matsushima, the Manbai, the Ichinao, and the Kusatsu. The owner of the Kusanoya had served as head clerk for the Kusatsu and was influential in the area. He married a former waitress and started their geisha house right behind the restaurant. In addition to hiring geisha who worked exclusively for the Kusanoya, the owner adopted O-Tome-chan and another girl, which showed he had intended to extend his business. But, in fact, he didn't devote much attention to it.

Though the couple knew the red-light district inside and out, they had not tasted the bitter experience of the world themselves. Therefore, whenever faced with a wealthy client's request to make one of their geisha his mistress, the couple hesitated. They could not bring themselves to force the girl's consent while fully aware that what they were doing was shameful. They would look at each other and decide not to broach the subject, murmuring, "That would be more than she can bear." I heard this kind of thing happened many times.

Furthermore, when young, the master of the house had acted like a would-be *soshi* [radical] and joined a social reform movement, but these activities frustrated him, so he changed to running a geisha house. This unusual background often made his actions incongruous. So when O-Tome-chan should have been taught the customs and necessary skills of a geisha, he also encouraged her to learn to read and write and repeatedly taught her that, in whatever situation, a human being, especially a woman, must not lose the purity of her heart or her thoughtfulness for others.

Be that as it may, O-Tome-chan acquired the general skills of her trade and started as an apprentice geisha under the name Jiro. She was in her thirteenth year by *kazoe-doshi** and had just finished a private elementary school. Naturally beautiful, this intelligent and cheerful apprentice geisha was popular in no time. The following year, her adoptive father died. At fifteen, when she became a full-fledged geisha, the master's wife said, "You must have a steady benefactor; it is the custom for geisha." O-Tome-chan responded firmly: "Oh, no, I won't do it!" Without hesitation she turned down the proposal. But the mistress of the house responded: "You say you won't, but remember, in this world . . ." The following words of her adoptive mother mixed with sighs, and finally she relented and pressed the girl no more. She could not be so hardhearted.

The expensive grand debut which she, as a geisha, was expected to make became a "family affair"—such a quiet one that she wore a senior geisha's banquet kimono that my aunt made over for the occasion. However, her modest debut, free of the conventions of the geisha world, rather heightened her popularity. O-Tome-chan, that is, the geisha Jiro, was now a popular figure sought by the gentlemen who frequented the Five Houses. She was known as the Asakusa geisha who entertained guests with her accomplishments and charming disposition alone.

Some among the men O-Tome-chan served courted her and tried to win her heart. But to them she said plainly and clearly, "I will not marry anyone who patronizes my services. A man who has lost his head over a geisha and marries her will soon go to other geishas in search of pleasure. Then the geisha, whose redemption was greatly celebrated when she became his wife, will return to her life as a geisha. Seeing such a woman makes me sad. I would not think of marrying a client. I will continue my life as a geisha." How wonderfully this bold, refreshing attitude reflected her woman's sense of honor!

It was Totaro-san, the young master of the Manseian, who finally captured O-Tome-chan's heart. He summoned her many times every month, and she found an irresistible pleasure in waiting on him. She overlooked the eleven years' difference in their ages and the fact that he was married. For the first time in her life, she fell in love with a man. She was in her seventeenth spring.

I suppose O-Tome-chan was attracted by Totaro-san's devotion to her and his refreshing Edokko disposition [a Tokyoite, that is, one who is liberal with money], as well as his handsome looks. With an amazed expression, the *okamisan* of the Kusanoya told my aunt that, at that time, O-Tome-chan exchanged letters with Totaro-san almost every day and waited on him cheerfully, like a girl from a respectable household. Yet she did not entertain the slightest idea of becoming his wife.

Their behavior continued for almost a year. One spring night Totaro-san said, "Living like this is too painful!" He couldn't stand the present state any longer. He said that he was going on a trip for some time. Totaro-san's words overwhelmed O-Tome-chan and left her speechless. To make matters worse, she discovered a small pistol hidden in his inside pocket—no one knew where he got it—and was seized with panic. With resolution she said, "If you kill yourself, I will kill myself with you!" So the couple embarked on a suicide trip, as if they were lovers in an Edo drama. To complete the drama O-Tome-chan was already pregnant.

"It was such a blow to the *okamisan* of the Kusanoya that for a time, she was laid up, totally dejected," my aunt whispered to Mother when this happened. Mother listened silently.

Under the full-blown cherry blossoms, the two wandered in search of a place for their death, drifting to a spa in Fukushima. Because of their joy in living together, they decided to live, at least until their child was born, thus wavering in their resolve to commit suicide. They finally rented an isolated cottage in a cherry orchard and began a solitary life there. On the levees of the rice fields, O-Tome-chan, sleeves gathered with a cord, picked Japanese parsley for their supper. She began to wish that they could continue this life for many years. The eighteen-year-old O-Tome-chan enjoyed every day of their life together—as if she were playing at housekeeping. At the touching sight of O-Tome-chan, happy in this lonely life, Totaro-san wrote to his sister telling her their whereabouts and seeking her help. O-Tome-chan gave birth to a boy here. Holding the baby and led by Totaro-san's sister, the two moved to the upstairs room of a friend's house in

Kameido. Soon after their move, the news of the unexpected death of Totaro-san's wife, who he had left at the Manseian, was brought to them.

✦ ✦ ✦

O-Tome-san was received into the Manseian as Totaro-san's second wife. This was solely the decision of the old master, Totaro-san's father, who heard the detailed story from his daughter. His wife had long been dead. Those were the days when, in all matters, formal distinctions were important. Totaro-san's first wife came from a family of the same trade and standing as the owner of the Manseian, and her death occurred while her husband and O-Tome-chan were living together. The old master had a hard time settling these matters with his late daughter-in-law's family.

One of my father's acquaintances, O-Miyo-san, was a maid in charge of housekeeping at the Manseian, and told my parents in later years, "The hard time the young mistress had then was unbearably painful to see." She added, "The wedding was—'humble' is not the right word—it was pitifully quiet. The mistress was lightly powdered, her hair done in a married woman's *marumage,* and wearing a striped kimono and a black *haori.* She kept her head bent all the time as if shrinking her lean body. Her normally attractive eyes suggested that she was brooding."

That was the day when O-Tome-san's hardship began. Her name was removed from the family register of her house of adoption, the geisha house, and also from that of her parents' home, the small candy shop. She was then adopted into a respectable house before her name was entered into her husband's family register. This was all arranged by the old master to maintain appearances of his restaurant. The young master, who had caused so much trouble for his family and for the shop, had to leave all these matters to his father and was in no position to say anything, however trivial. Nor was O-Tome-san to know the contents of the gifts she personally gave to the many employees on her wedding day. Some of the older maids and the cooks scorned her from the beginning: "Hah! The bride who brought nothing but her baggage. . ." "A former geisha mistress . . . let's bet on how long she can bear it." The grand restaurant was filled with such blunt backbiting and whining.

A young woman, knowing nothing but the world of a geisha, suddenly enters a respectable household as, of all things, the mistress of a long-established restaurant—recalling the time, O-Miyo-san whispered to us, "Honestly, I was afraid the burden would be too much for her to carry." But the day after the wedding, O-Tome-san, sleeves tucked up, diligently polished the trays piled up before her. On seeing O-Tome-san's laudable behavior, O-Miyo-san said, she shed tears of sympathy.

Once he had returned to his own home, the lover, for whom O-Tome-san had risked her life, unmistakably became the young master of the house. He was born a diligent worker and loved his trade. His position did not allow him to appear to be overly pleasant to his wife before his employees. So he occasionally scolded her harshly, saying such things as "Don't ask me so many questions. Use your brain. How can your husband help you in everything you do?" Then, to emphasize this coldness, he turned away from her. But he didn't really mean what he had said.

When the brothers of the late wife came to the Manseian for a meeting of their trade, they too were different. A short time before, they and O-Tome-san had been cheerful guests and a popular geisha, enjoying themselves as they exchanged witty remarks and jokes. But now the former guests wore chilled expressions. Tradesmen who did business with the Manseian smiled at her amiably and politely addressed her as "Madam." But beneath this facade, they were contemptuous. This was obvious to everybody.

Exhausted from being attentive in all areas, the girl, who had a delicate body to begin with, quickly lost weight. But O-Tome-san's countenance was never dark or sad. She was always cheerful and amiable, and this made her all the more pitiful.

One day about two months after the simple wedding, O-Miyo-san woke at dawn and went to the lavatory. She was frightened to see the mistress standing expressionless in the still gloomy garden. O-Miyo-san called to her. O-Tome-san slowly turned back and smiled. "Another day is dawning," she said and returned to her room. Moved by this pathetic figure, O-Miyo-san then resolved to do anything in her power for the mistress.

Totaro-san's sister O-Ryu-san took every opportunity to pay respect to O-Tome-san as her elder sister-in-law, addressing her, appropriately, as "Sister." In confidence, she revealed that she was aware of how important O-Tome-san was to her brother: "Whatever happens, I pray that you will never leave my brother. If that should happen, he is sure to kill himself this time. Please promise!" O-Ryu-san's heartfelt words must have bolstered O-Tome-san's spirit.

So it went for half a year. Finally the family saw a day when the old master and his son chatted over trivial matters, laughing cheerfully, for the first time in the past few years. The sustained effort of the young mistress had finally begun to restore harmony to their domestic dissonance. Her admirable and wholehearted pains, without complaint, to become the *okamisan* of a *soba* shop—this sincerity of the young mistress was like a spring wind which softly enveloped the household.

In her early days at the Manseian, O-Tome-san's deportment often provoked the old master's frowns. When he could no longer contain himself, he said with uncharacteristic formality, "Come here a minute, O-Tome," and led her into a back room. This happened immediately after she greeted her husband on his coming home by standing and nodding her head in an enticing manner while greeting him.

"O-Tome, you are the *okamisan* of this restaurant. Flirtatious gestures are unacceptable. Greet all who enter on your knees and with a bow. Look! Like this." So saying, the father-in-law demonstrated the correct posture by laying both his hands on the *tatami* floor and saying, "Make a triangle with the index fingers and the thumbs of both hands, and bow by putting your nose to it, so to speak."

She followed his demonstration to the letter. "I'm sorry, Father," she said. "Is this the way?" So saying, she practiced bowing again and again like a primary school girl. O-Miyo-san said she saw O-Tome-san doing this from behind the sliding screen and could not help uttering, "What an adorable girl!" The old master was also pleased. After this, whenever O-Tome-san pleased him, he said, "Ah, what innocence! What a blessing to have such a daughter-in-law!" Then, the old master taught her how to offer morning and evening greetings, how to receive a guest, and how to contend with the minute details a cashier encounters. The mistress learned them, one after another, like paper absorbing water.

Before they knew it, the employees found themselves siding with the mistress. In those days, restaurants provided resident employees with *yono** *butons* [thick, quilted bedding, slightly over four feet wide] with which to cover themselves. One of the employees often repeated the story of how the mistress replaced his thinly stuffed bedding with soft and comfortable bedding. He was unimaginably happy and praised her kindness profusely. After that, none of the young kitchen workers spoke ill of her.

In the course of ten years, O-Tome-san gave birth to five children, two of them born dead. However, her great concern at the time was her husband's health. He was frail by nature and was always catching cold. He discovered that he had contracted tuberculosis, a disease very much dreaded at that time. Because of his trade, the family feared that revealing his illness and his hospitalization would affect the shop's reputation. The most he could do was to go away secretly for a change of air, the treatment in those days.

When the Great Kanto Earthquake struck, the young master was in Hakone. All his family were safe, but the old master, the pillar of the household, died in the makeshift house they had built. O-Tome-san's frantic efforts enabled her to keep the business going, but because she had no man to supervise the house, she often cried to the late master at the family altar, "Help me, Father, please!"

When O-Tome-san was thirty, Totaro-san died, in spite of her caring for him night and day. While holding his beloved wife's hands, his last words were "I was a lucky man." O-Miyo-san wept in sympathy at her young mistress' grief. "The young master must have thanked God for having such a dedicated wife," O-Miyo-san said when she told the touching story of O-Tome-san's devotion.

Although the mistress was distraught, talk was already bubbling on the lips of people about her. Who would be the family heir? The eldest son of the first wife? O-Tome-san's three boys? Totaro-san's younger brother Rokuro-san, said to be the old master's favorite son? He had left home after O-Tome-san came to the Manseian. The old master said until his last day, "How I wish Rokuro were home! I wonder why he wanders so." The master's grief was endless.

Depressed by the family's discussions of these difficult problems and lured by her former geisha friends, O-Tome-san found herself, at one time, inclined to return to the world of the geisha. But the thought of her three sons and her lack of confidence in her skills as a geisha made her decide to follow her relatives' advice and marry Rokuro-san.

O-Tome-san had a more important reason for this decision. She learned that she was the cause of Rokuro-san's wandering, though she had never suspected it before. Rokuro-san had fallen in love with her when she was introduced to him as his sister-in-law ten-odd years before. He was unable to shake off his longing for her and, in his suffering, left home and began to wander.

O-Miyo-san said, "I somehow suspected it when I saw how Rokuro-san behaved on the rare occasions that he came home—like a spoiled child. The mistress, a naive woman, reprimanded her brother-in-law, who was one year older than she, as if she were his real sister: 'What complaints do you have? Stop your roaming and come home now.'"

The reason Rokuro-san had not come home to see his brother on his deathbed was that Totaro-san had discovered some of Rokuro-san's scribbling that revealed his love for his sister-in-law. Rokuro-san despised himself for what he had done and thought that no apology to his brother could suffice. When her marriage to her brother-in-law was decided, O-Tome-san had her name withdrawn from the family register. In this way, she, with three children of her own, forfeited her rights and married Rokuro-san, who was then the heir of the house. O-Tome-san desired this arrangement in order not to hurt her second husband's pride.

When Rokuro-san showed her a haiku he had written for her, the dear mistress, as a woman, must have thanked God for her happiness:

> In all of Japan
> I am the most happy man—
> The moon in summer!

I am told that she devoted herself to her second husband.

✦ ✦ ✦

Two years after this, the Manseian was suddenly forced from Okuyama. In the court trial concerning the lease of land after the expiration of the contract, the Senso-ji temple, the landlord, won its suit against the Tokyo City Government, the tenant. The Manseian, which subleased its land from the city government, was forced to leave. The relatives consulted, but to them protesting the court ruling was out of the question. The phrase "the tenant's right of residence" was probably unknown in those days.

The new land they barely managed to obtain in Umamichi was about twenty-nine *tsubo,* less than one-tenth of the three-hundred *tsubo* of Okuyama. The family and relatives were too dejected to shed tears, they say. Yet the mistress took heart and encouraged Rokuro-san so that they could provide the same excellent fare as before, even though the restaurant was much smaller.

According to O-Miyo-san, Rokuro-san was away from home when he should have learned the trade, so, unlike his brother, he knew little about the business. And his pride did not allow him to ask the experienced men of his shop to teach him about the selection of buckwheat flour, the knack of kneading the flour, and the right flavor of the broth. It must have been difficult for Rokuro-san to see these men and the maids going over his head for advice from O-Tome-san. The greater her devotion, the more guilty he felt toward his late brother and the greater his suffering from his loss of confidence. He had once experienced a nervous break-down from which he had completely recovered. But he had a relapse. And this one was worse. One day about three years after their move to Umamichi, soon after O-Miyo-san resigned under some unavoidable circumstances, Rokuro-san suddenly died. He was thirty-four years old.

When the war became more intense and buckwheat flour was impossible to obtain, however hard the mistress and her employees searched for it, the Manseian of such long standing finally closed. Soon after that, the building burned in an air raid. No trace of it remains. O-Tome-san must now be in her late seventies. I hear she looks ten years younger, with fair skin, a thick and short body, and eyes as clear and beautiful as ever. Two of her children, fathered by Totaro-san, died of illness, and one was killed in the war. She and Rokuro-san had two sons. The younger son, Koji, who has a good business head, runs a *soba* shop called "Okuyama" in Ogura. His elder brother ran a fancy *sushi* shop called "Sushicho" in Roppongi and did good business, which pleased his mother. Unfortunately, he died some time ago. Now his shop is managed by his employees. O-Tome-san only occasionally appears in her sons' shops. Thanks to the reputation of her shop, her sons' shops are prospering, patronized by young movie and TV personalities and middle-aged guests.

✦ ✦ ✦

Here we see an Asakusa woman who lived a life with no regrets. She loved and was loved by those dear to her for seventy years. I heartily wish to bestow my blessing on the remaining years of this woman, Mrs. Tome Hirano, who has had all a woman's blessings from heaven.

A Little Fig Lover

 Our house in Saruwaka-machi had a garden covering less than three *tsubo** [about twelve square yards], and at its corner by the lavatory grew a fig tree of a considerable size. The tree bore much sweet fruit every summer. My father didn't like fruit, then called *mizugashi* [juicy cake]. He showed no interest whatsoever in our figs, saying, "How can I eat anything from a tree growing near a filthy place?" Like Father, neither of my brothers cared for figs. So Mother and I monopolized them, and we could eat as many as we liked every year.

If the figs were on a branch too high for us to reach, we plucked them off with a two-pronged pole we used for drying clothes and put them into a basket. We also counted the figs on the tree with our eyes, thinking to ourselves, "This one here and that one there will be good for eating tomorrow." If, the next day, the birds had pecked these ripe figs, we stamped our feet in anger. When it rained hard, we worried that the rain might damage the fragile ripe fruit.

Even now, when I happen to see figs at a fruit shop, I sometimes succumb to the temptation to buy them, forgetting that I might be on my way to a wedding. Yet these figs, arranged in beautiful white boxes, which were displayed with a variety of choice fruit, don't taste very good: When the figs are cut in two, the red flesh becomes dry, with no sticky sweetness. Whenever I buy them, I am disappointed.

As she put the amber, almost transparent flesh of one

of our figs into her mouth, Mother used to say, "This is 'white fig,' a rare variety." Of the white milky sap that dripped from the spot from which a fig was plucked, she would say, "This is good for getting rid of the worms that live in your stomach. Because you eat figs, you will have no worms." "And if you boil the large leaves in water," she said, "you can apply the mixture to prickly heat and cure it." We did dry those leaves in the shade and then boiled them, and I, who perspired profusely, bathed in a tub filled with this water.

When I was young, I was indeed a "fig child."

The Miyato Theater

 To young Asakusa girls, seeing plays at the Miyato Theater was a greater pleasure than anything else. The masters of merchant households strictly warned their young daughters and other female employees against going out alone or seeking entertainment at night and didn't allow them to go to movies, but these masters didn't object to them going to the Miyato. The masters looked forward to a new program and frequently said in good humor, "It's a long time since I saw *Kagotsurube* [a Kabuki play recounting the love story of a farmer and a courtesan]. It's always good." Reflecting their enthusiasm, these men supported their favorite actors with gifts. The plays performed in this small theater were full of charm and vigor, yet suggested good manners, and the hardworking people of the area welcomed them. Undoubtedly, the stage of the Miyato was always lively, merry, and enjoyable.

Young actors, strictly trained by their seniors who were proud of their skill, put their heart and soul into their work. Solid performances made them popular and brought them good roles and subsequently more money. These rewards encouraged them. Actors who performed in the major theaters scorned these Asakusa actors, with remarks such as "Who would want to perform in such a small theater as Asakusa's?" or "What can you expect from 'penny-theater' actors?" But the people of Asakusa thought that the performances at the Miyato were more attractive than the plays performed by the foremost actor families who rested on their prestige. I believe these plays stirred the very souls of the people of Asakusa.

When the new play for the month began, shop masters, the house regulars, and geisha from the area filled the boxes on both sides of the stage. Teahouse waitresses busily served them tea and lunches. The railed-off sections before the stage had been replaced by rows of chairs, and in came people such as a fishmonger's wife wearing a *haori* [a formal halfcoat] who managed the time to see the play, or a young man employed in a liquor shop who removed his apron for the occasion. A new arrival might say, "Excuse me, would you mind making a little room for me?" A person already seated might say, "Oh, yes, young man, I can make some room." So saying, each moved by turns for new arrivals. During the intermissions vendors with boxes hanging from their shoulders came strolling between the rows, crying, "Hey, rice crackers, caramels. Take your pick. How about some peanuts and lemon pop?" Those who planned to see the entire play, and some lasted until evening, treated themselves to a packet of *sushi.*

Once I saw a young man in the audience with his mouth stuffed with a *norimaki sushi* [vinegared rice wrapped in *nori,* processed seaweed]. He was absorbed by the action of the play, as his favorite actor moved in perfect harmony with the accompanying beat of clappers. At a climactic moment, the young man, without thinking, shouted "Daitooryoo!" [in some circumstances, the equivalent of "Bravo!"]. As he did, a piece of sushi caught in his throat, and his eyes began to roll. Someone a short distance away shouted, "Pull yourself together, young man!" And the whole house burst into laughter. Such incidents were common at the Miyato Theater.

✦ ✦ ✦

When my younger brother debuted as a Kabuki actor at age five, the Miyato was in its best days, with the performance of popular actors like Komasaburo Matsumoto, Denjiro Sawamura, and Kigan Ichikawa. I was three years older than my brother and became his attendant in place of my mother, so in my primary school days, I went to the Miyato every day after school. Once offstage, my brother, playful boy that he was, ran around or fell asleep in a "house" on stage left. So I, his attendant, had to keep a watchful eye on him.

I taught him *origami,* to fold pieces of paper so they resembled cranes, footmen, and the like. Or I told him

fairy tales in a low voice behind the set. I was determined to keep him entertained. Sometimes I was so
absorbed in telling these stories that we missed an
important scene in which my brother was to appear.
When that happened, the greenroom manager would
tap me lightly on my head and say sternly, "What are
you here for, young lady?"

Even at such times, Kigan Ichikawa, the leading actor
of female roles, was kind to me. "There's no need to cry,
Tei-bo," he said. "Just be more careful next time, okay?"
At the height of his popularity, with a handsome
appearance and an aquiline nose and his acting skill
acknowledged, Ichikawa-san was kind enough to give
my brother a role whenever a child was needed in
Sendaihagi or *Shigenoi* [famous Kabuki plays in which a
child has an important role. See chap. 24]. Whenever
patrons sent confections to the greenroom in appreciation of his fine performance, Ichikawa-san called to us,
"Tei-bo, Toku-bo, come here a minute. I have something for you!" I liked him best of all the actors, and
wishing to help him, I scurried about to tidy his dressing table, unfortunately sometimes hindering his pupils.

✦ ✦ ✦

When I saw him recently after a long interval,
Ichikawa-san recalled, "You used to change my water for
powdering, Tei-bo." In addressing me, a woman in her
late sixties, he still called me "Tei-bo"—as if I were a
child [see "Address" in the Glossary.]. In his later career,
"Uncle" Kigan was selected by the great actor Kikugoro
Onoe* the Sixth to play the role of his wife, assuming
the name Taganojo Onoe.

"Uncle" Kigan is now in his ninetieth year of *kazoe**, and his highly trained performance, that of the greatest contemporary player of old women, still gives a thrilling pleasure to theatergoers. Yet the Miyato Theater, which entertained the Shitamachi people so much, is gone. No trace whatsoever remains.

The District Around the Hanayashiki

On the right side of the road leading to Rokku [an administrative unit comparable to a ward] from the Kannon Hall of the Senso-ji temple is the Hanayashiki [the flower estate], facing the site of the former Gourd Pond. Much earlier, as I heard the old people say, it was a beautiful garden for admiring flowers in each season, and *tanka* and *haiku* poets held meetings there. Later, the garden became an amusement park for children, because, as I was told, the increasing number of movie houses and theaters eventually turned the adjacent Rokku into an amusement quarters. The Hanayashiki could no longer be maintained as a garden for people of refined taste. Now it is a lively amusement park with a variety of rides. In my days it was also, in its way, a good place for amusement.

In my childhood, the admission at the Hanayashiki was five *sen* for an adult, two or three *sen* for a child [a sen was .01 yen]. In the spacious grounds where I went to play were mounds, artificial waterfalls, and large red *higoi* [decorative fish of various colors, related to carp] swimming in the pond. In cages, here and there, were monkeys, foxes, pheasants, and peacocks, making that corner of the grounds a small zoo. On a small stage just beyond the zoo area, a well-trained blue titmouse walked a tightrope while carrying a prophesy written on a piece of paper in its bill. I never tired of watching its unvarying movement. The puppet theater next to the bird's stage was always crowded with children. Plays based on such fairy tales as "*Momotaro*" ["The Peach Boy"], "The Monkey-Crab Fight," and "The Sparrow Whose Tongue Was Cut" were presented with puppets smaller than those in Bunraku* shows. Children screamed with horror when, by some contrivances, one-eyed fiends and paper-umbrella monsters rose slowly from a large wicker basket which the greedy old woman brought in "The Sparrow Whose Tongue Was Cut."

Scenes from famous plays, represented by lifelike dolls, were always on display on the stage near the entrance facing Rokku. In the autumn the dolls were dressed in chrysanthemums. Many people came from great distances to see the chrysanthemum dolls made by Mr. Kamehachi Yasumoto, who lived in Asakusa and who was known for his masterly skill. In particular, a large crowd always gathered before the grand doll of Oishi Kuranosuke* [the famous leader of a band of forty-seven warriors] in the twelve different scenes from the play *Chushingura.*

Outside the Hanayashiki, lean-to stalls lined a hundred-meter wall that faced the Gourd Pond. These street stalls catered to customers from rural areas. A sale on kitchen gadgets was heralded by a poster with bold handwriting, "Great New Inventions." One was for peeling radishes and another named the "civilization knife" was for cutting a carrot in the shape of a plum flower. At another stall, an old-clothes dealer displayed a man's *haori* [a half coat] with family crests, a woman's *obi* sash of mousseline delaine [a high-grade worsted woolen fabric], and padded sleeveless kimono jackets, underclothing, and *haragake** [backless vests] for children. Such businesses seemed to prosper in those days.

✦ ✦ ✦

It was the time when I had just entered primary school. I took my younger brother Tokunosuke one day to see the chrysanthemum dolls. One secondhand dealer displayed hanging scrolls on which Mount Fuji or a crane and a pine tree were painted or offered figurines of Hotei and Daikoku, two of the Seven Deities of Fortune.

In front of the stall, a soldier was shouting at the stallkeeper, "How can you call yourself a Japanese subject? Bite your tongue and kill yourself, you unpatriotic scoundrel." Some stars on his shoulder epaulets indicated that the soldier was a private first class or a master sergeant. His flushed face was that of a young man. Lying prostrate at his feet, the secondhand dealer was begging his pardon. This dealer usually squatted cross-legged by his shop, pipe in mouth. Whenever children sat on their heels before his articles, he was mean and shouted, "Get out of here, you brats. This is no place for you." He was a swarthy man, and children were afraid of him.

A curious crowd had already gathered, but stood at a distance. Awed by the soldier's overpowering attitude, nobody spoke. Even my brother and I immediately saw that the cause of the trouble was a photograph of the Emperor and the Empress that stood beside the dealer. In those days Their Majesties' portrait in a frame was a popular souvenir for country people. One was always displayed at this stall, but customarily, pieces of white paper covered each of the faces of the royal couple. Everyone understood that, although such sales were permitted on the street, Their Majesties' faces must be covered. Exposing them was considered disrespectful.

The problem arose because in the course of the portrait being taken in and out daily, the fastening of the paper had become weak, and the strong wind that day had blown one of the pieces away. So His Majesty's face was exposed. Apparently, the stallkeeper had failed to notice this. He repeatedly apologized to the soldier, saying that, as a Japanese citizen, he was very sorry for his oversight. At long last, his desperate begging for forgiveness must have calmed the soldier's anger. As the soldier left, he said, "If you ever do that again, I won't forgive you, man!" With sweat beading on his forehead, the stallkeeper was relieved to see the soldier retreating. Unlike the man who frightened children, he was a different person—timid and nervous.

On the way home after enjoying a puppet show, Tokunosuke and I passed the same dealer's stall. The man was then quite calm and was seated, pipe in mouth, as usual, but he looked crestfallen, perhaps because he was sitting straight on the straw mat, with his knees neatly placed together under his baggy trousers. For some reason he was not sitting on his usually dirty cushion. Then I saw a frame wrapped in wrinkled, arabesque-patterned cloth sitting beside him on the cushion. "Look! I'm sure that parcel in the wrapper is Their Majesties' portrait," I whispered to my brother, and we left the spot quickly.

After this incident, no framed portrait of Their Majesties appeared again at this stall. As always, the man was seated cross-legged on his thin cushion, pipe in mouth, scolding children who stood before his shop. However, hanging by his stall, where the august, framed portrait had been, was an old scroll, picturing a tiger, like a cat, peering from a bamboo grove.

Dobucho-san

 In the days when our house was at Umamichi, my elder brother, Tomokazu, was eight or nine, I think. I was three years younger, the middle child. My younger brother, Tokunosuke, was three years younger than I. While taking care of us, Mother attended to my father and managed the household, so she was always a whirl of activity. Whenever she heard the children next door crying frantically, however, she would stop everything and rush to them murmuring, "There they go again." As I recall, the husband next door was never home. His wife, a woman of twenty-four or -five, was small and slim and already the mother of three children. Moreover, the last two were born in successive years. Without relatives to help, her hands were full, and when she couldn't control her temper, she sometimes slapped her children.

On such an occasion, Mother would go to the woman and gently chide her: "Slapping them on the head so often will make them dull." "Now, let me see," she said, taking a baby from the wife's hands and unfolding its diaper. "Look, his bottom is sore. No baby cries without cause. Your other baby is just crying to keep this one company. Everything's OK with him, so don't worry." Turning to the oldest, Mother said, "You're hungry, aren't you, big boy? Come to our house. We have some good rice crackers for you." While doing this, she took a pot of burned taro roots from the stove. Mother clucked her tongue and said, "See what you have done. Well, why don't you boil some tofu for the evening?" Giving the wife tips on that evening's meal, Mother came home holding the eldest child by the hand.

On another occasion, Mother prepared extra fried vegetables so we could share with the woman and her children. Another time, while teaching the young mother how to stuff bedclothes with cotton, Mother listened to the wife's complaints about her husband, who had not been home for three days.

My mother may have appeared to be a busybody, but she thought it quite proper for a mature woman with housekeeping experience to look after a young wife with many children. To begin with, Mother saw it as a token of goodwill toward our neighbor. "She's our neighbor, isn't she?" Mother would say. With that in mind, she was always willing to help and never seemed put out when her help was needed.

Come to think of it, women nicknamed "Dobucho" lived on most alleys of Asakusa. These wives were frank, strong-minded, and liked to take care of others. The origin of that term is curious. Once in the early Edo period [1603–1868], in Hanakawado-cho, on the bank of the Sumida River, an *oyabun* [a great person] once lived, an employment agent named Banzuiin Chobei. His actions became so legendary that he is now a popular Kabuki figure. When trouble among honest, hardworking townspeople drove them to their wits' end, this boss, a stout man, came on the scene with deliberation and, risking his own life, settled the matter. The people adored him and called him *"oyabun."*

In Mother's time, though lacking the dignity of Banzuiin Chobei, an officious wife would run out rattling the board cover of a drainage ditch, a *dobu*, to help her neighbors in trouble, so people combined the words and nicknamed such a woman "Dobucho-san." If something needed attention in her neighborhood, a *dobucho*, neglecting the affairs of her own household, said, "Leave it to me. I'll settle the problem to your advantage." Striking her chest as a symbol of her resolve, she did her best to find a solution.

Some people said scornfully that while the meddlesome wife struck her chest, she didn't strike her purse to empty it, as the real Chobei-san had done. They said, "She's just a busybody! How brazen of her to let people think of her as a Chobei-san." Yet these women were good-hearted and acted with good intentions. They might respond, "We should help each other when we are in trouble." People knew this conviction well, so, though sometimes the *dobucho*'s goodwill went too far and she became a nuisance, they still went to her with their problems. They, in turn, took some action, if only a small and negligible one, to help others in trouble.

In the Asakusa of those days, life would not have gone smoothly without such mutual help. We had no men of great wealth or influence, only good-natured, common people without power who lived huddled together, so to speak. Therefore we needed strong individuals to intervene in the affairs of others.

My mother was one of these *dobucho.*

Otori-sama:
The Festival of the Rooster

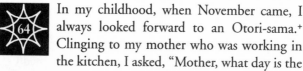 In my childhood, when November came, I always looked forward to an Otori-sama.[+] Clinging to my mother who was working in the kitchen, I asked, "Mother, what day is the *ichi-no-tori* [the first day of the rooster]?" Taking an

---

[+]See "O-" and "Sama" under "Address, forms of" in the Glossary. The rooster is the tenth of the twelve Chinese zodiac symbols, which start with the rat and end with the wild boar. Each day in the month has one symbol assigned to it in this order. See *junishi* in the Glossary.

almanac from a drawer in the *nagahibachi* [an oblong ceramic container holding hot coals for heating a room; the small drawers hold frequently used items], she found the date for me. The days of the rooster in November were festival days of the Otori Shrine near Yoshiwara [until 1958, the government-licensed red-light district], and in the evening large crowds flocked to the fair held in the precincts. The first day of the rooster was called *ichi-no-tori* and the second, *ni-no-tori*. If November had a third day of the rooster, the day was called *san-no-tori* [*ichi, ni, san,* that is, "first, second, third"]. If such a day occurred, we were warned that more fires than usual would break out that year.

Every year, on the evening of Otori-sama I was anxious for my father, a great lover of festivals, to say to us, "Want to come along with me to the festival?" My little brother and I would change our clothes long before the evening, bring out our new clogs, and wait eagerly.

On the evening of *ichi-no-tori* in my fourth or fifth year of primary school, my father returned home from work and urged us to get ready. Excited and finishing dinner quickly, my brother and I scrambled to open the door first. As we were stepping out, Sho-san's wife ran to our house, her face pale, her hair disheveled. "I bet she and her husband are having another fight," my brother said. "We're out of luck!" I said. "On the evening of Otori-sama. May this session soon be over," I prayed. Complaining, my brother and I waited in the living room for father to come and take us to the festival. But our hopes were dashed. Late that night, the couple decided to divorce, paying no attention to my father's advice against it.

Sho-san was a minor Kabuki actor and was already over thirty. He was a quiet man of imposing stature and rather ugly, but Father liked him because of his ability to fight well on stage. He was a playboy who drank, gambled, and frequented brothels. His wife, ten years younger than he, worked as a maid at a *gyuya* [a restaurant specializing in beef] and was never free from the tears of a broken heart. They had been married for five years. Having no relatives, they came to my father when their quarrels got out of control. Until then, they had resolved their differences with my father's help, but that time, it seemed, his wife could stand it no longer.

When Father took us to the following *ni-no-tori* fair, twelve days later, the couple's divorce had slipped my mind. Walking from Saruwaka-machi through Umamichi, through the Fuji Alley to Senzoku-machi and finally to the riverbank, we passed under the roof of the Ōmon Gate of Yoshiwara. People streamed along— children with the tips of their noses red from the cold and aged people wrapped in woolen shawls all walked on, laughing merrily.

I wonder now why it was so cold at that time. Though only November, everybody was sniffling and kept their hands in their sleeves. We looked like *yakko-dako* [kites shaped like stylized footmen with hands covered by their sleeves]—we had no hands. Running through the crowd, young men in winter kimonos but no undershirts cried in high-pitched voices, "Clear the way! Clear the way!"

Passing through Nakano-cho, we glanced at the *hikitejaya* [restaurants where men could arrange contracts with prostitutes] with their colorful lanterns hanging from the eaves and at the photographs of women from the brothels. Then we came to a street jammed with rows of stalls. A young man wearing the work coat of his shop and a towel around his head was swinging around a cord with red, white, and green rice cakes tied to it and shouting in a lively voice, "Hey! I've got *mochi,* right here. If you want to be an *ōgane-mochi,* get your *mochi* here [a pun on *mochi,* meaning "rice cake" and "man"]!"

In the next stall, a well-dressed old man was putting pieces of *kirizansho* [a cake made of rice powder and seasoned with sugar and *sansho,* an aromatic spice] into small bags. This soft cake that tasted like *suama* [a steamed rice powder cake without *sansho*] was my favorite. Another stall sold *tonoimo,* five big round steamed taro roots skewered on a stalk of bamboo tied at both ends to form a circle. Eating *tonoimo* was said to make you *to* [a leader], perhaps because the words contain the same sound.

The chief attraction of the Otori-sama Fair was the sale of ornamental rakes, ranging from one so tiny it could be hidden in the palm of the hand to one as large as a *tatami* mat [3' x 6']. The rakes were made of bamboo and decorated with all the happy symbols—the Seven Deities of Good Fortune, the crane and the tortoise, *okame* [a round-faced woman's mask], and others with a charm of the Otori Shrine in the center. Such a rake, said to gather good luck, was an indispensable ornament for businesses related to geisha and to the world of pleasure. Every time a large rake was sold, the dealers all clapped their hands vigorously and shouted,

"Yooi, yoyoyoi, yoyoyoi, yoi." The customer went on his way, all smiles, as if he had already raked in a fortune.

As the night advanced, the precincts of the Otori Shrine became as crowded and noisy as a fight scene, so congested that many devout men and women could not get near enough to toss coins into the offertory chests. So they threw their coins from some distance with all their might and, with their palms together in front of their faces, prayed for good luck in the coming year. Children scampered about at their feet, picking up offerings that had missed the chests and fallen to the ground. Only on that night was it *not* considered a sin to pocket money given as an offering. Instead, doing so was considered an attempt to "catch" good fortune. So parents connived to let the children do it.

I held Father's sleeve tightly so as not to lose sight of him. As we came out of the crowded precincts to take a shortcut home by way of Shibasaki-cho, I saw a stall standing alone by the roadside selling *ōgane-mochi.* I then cried out in surprise. In front of the stall stood our Sho-san. Snuggling against the back of his tall body, happy smiles on her rosy cheeks, and joking with the young stallkeeper was none other than his wife, who was to have parted from her husband forever on the night of *ichi-no-tori.* When I pointed to the scene, my father roughly grabbed my hand and pushed it down, and shook his head. Then he strode away.

"What's up? What's the matter, Sis?" asked my brother inquisitively.

I took his hand and said, "Nothing. Nothing at all." We hurried after my father, my face down, as if I had done something wrong.

What became of Sho-san and his wife after that, I don't know.

A Dragonfly in Paradise

 Yone-san, whom my father helped enlist in the Kabuki troupe as a costumer during its tour of Kyushu, brought him a souvenir, a talisman. "This one works wonders! I mean it," he said. "A penniless old man confined himself in the shrine dedicated to this god and offered prayers for one entire night. After that, he made a fortune by speculating in the rice market. If you pray to the god of this talisman, you are sure to make money."

Without even pausing to wipe his broad, sweaty forehead, Yone-san took the talisman reverently from his small, wrapped bundle. His talk was as detailed as if he had witnessed the old man's story. Yet, when Father asked in amusement, "Is that so? And what's the name of the god?" Yone-san was suddenly at a loss. "Well, let me see. What was the name, I wonder? Isn't it written on the talisman? How does this read, please?" Yone-san was always like that.

As was the custom, property men and costumers brought back trinkets from tours and gave them as souvenirs. They usually bought my father a talisman of a god or a Buddha. Though not very religious, my father liked talismans. Everybody knew that he appreciated talismans of any deity. Most were inexpensive, so they were handy souvenirs.

Nobu-san the stagehand once brought Father a talisman from a shrine in Gifu and spoke of its powers: "Between you and me and the gatepost, this miraculous talisman makes you popular with women. It really works wonders. As a matter of fact, with its help, I . . ." he said, making sheep's eyes. He was about to continue, but then noticed Mother, who was making tea beside them. "Oh, no, you don't need this one. You're already too popular with women. How about this one? It protects you from harm." "I'll be happy to take both," Father said immediately, and that settled it.

As a result of such gifts, our household altar contained rows of talismans, one next to another, from shrines and temples all over the country. On the first and the fifteenth of every month, we offered at the altar rice boiled with *adzuki* beans and red and white *daifuku* [rice cakes stuffed with bean jam]. Every morning, after dressing, Father's practice was to light a candle and offer a long prayer. He mumbled in a high-pitched voice, but I had no idea whether it was a Shinto prayer or a sutra. But I understood certain phrases clearly. They were his appeals, uttered intermittently, concerning worries in his real life. "Please, please help fill the Miyato Theater." "Please help Kunitaro (my elder brother's stage name) perform his first role of Osome well."

It was fun to see that, while praying fervently, Father never failed to reproach Mother or me. He was exactly like Kobei the scolder in *Rakugo,* a comic story. "Pray . . . mumble, mumble . . . Say, Tei-bo, can't you make tea properly? You're a girl, aren't you? Remember the tea you made last night? It was like horse's urine . . . mumble, mumble." "Pray, by the great power of the Great Shrine of Ise . . . Say, Mother, put plenty of ingredients in the miso soup this morning. Eating *wakame* [seaweed] for two days running makes my stomach smell of the sea . . . mumble, mumble . . . Pray, if you grant my wish, I will contribute a great *torii** [post and lintel arches on the paths of Shinto shrines] this time, for sure . . . mumble, mumble."

Once I mentioned that donating a great *torii* seemed to be an overstatement, to which my father replied, "Don't be foolish. A lie is sometimes expedient, they say. And an exaggerated lie is better than a modest one. The gods will be pleased with my prayers and say, 'Extraordinary! I'll overlook your extravagance.' That's where gods prove themselves to be generous." We laughed until our sides ached.

When I asked which of the numberless talismans was the most effective, Father answered: "It's hard to say which, as hard as to tell *ayame* from *kakitsubata* [two species of iris]. The world being as it is, gods have a hard time listening to all our prayers. They have too many to answer. If I pray to all the gods together every day, some time or other some one of them will manage to grant my wish."

Father's attitude toward the gods was so casual that it deserved punishment. But his wishes were never greedy, disproportionate to his means and status. I also never heard him utter such selfish wishes, such as "Pray help me make a fortune," or "Pray help my daughter marry a millionaire." This is where his virtue lay. Though he was flirtatious and always had his way before his wife, he was frank, like men with Edokko* [literally, a person from Tokyo, but various positive and negative qualities are associated with the term], and his personal charms made him likable. So I suppose the gods must have pardoned him.

My father spent his entire life in the world of the stage where people lived in a happy-go-lucky way. But he never made mistakes in money matters and was the last person to cause others financial grief. He used to say, "Confound it! I could never act so shamefully!" He died not long after the end of the war at the age of eighty-four, and I think his life was a moderately happy one.

Perhaps in the world beyond, father is a "dragonfly in paradise," a flippant, happy-go-lucky fellow who, favored by gods, flits from place to place and talks about beautiful women, forgetting the passage of time. So I, his daughter, believe.

The Rag Shop

 Behind the park near my home was the shop of a rag dealer. In front of her shop, which was six feet wide, with low eaves, hung scraps of cloth of various colors—pretty Yuzen silk crepe, chic striped silk crepe, red silk, black *habutae* silk—pieces from six inches to two feet at most.

The geisha and people of the pleasure district would send whole rolls of cloth, about nine yards, for tailoring without estimating how much was needed. What remained of the roll after cutting was the seamstress's gain. She sold these odd pieces to the rag dealer, who, in turn, sold them for a profit in her shop. Young girls spent all their allowances to buy the pieces they liked and make themselves handbags and purses. Occasionally they made luxurious aprons.

In front of the rag shop, the colorful cloth resembled the strips of fancy paper hanging from bamboo branches during Tanabata, the Star Festival. Among these fragments, we could see the lean proprietress of the shop, sitting quietly. Although she was no longer a girl, she had an aura of grace about her. However, she sat stiffly and always with a blank stare as she aimlessly passed time by using tongs to level the ashes in a small *hibachi* [a charcoal-burning heater or stove]. Every time I saw her, she had a cloth on her temples to cure a headache. I'm told her husband was given to gambling.

The Girl with a Ribbon in Her Hair

 With a smile on her face, Shimeko-san stood at my door. I noticed that she looked almost the same as she did when she was a girl. She had wound her jaunty woolen shawl around her neck, with one end jutting up at the back, just as she had done when she was the most fashionable girl in the primary school we attended. Was it nearly fifty years since I had had a long easy chat with her? She must have had many experiences during those years, but I was glad to find she bore the same gentle expression of her youth and still had her habit of speaking slowly, while tilting her head a bit.

Shimeko-san was the only child of the owner of the roller-skating rink in Rokku, Asakusa, and was the heart of her parents' love. Once, seven or eight of our classmates and I were invited to her home for her birthday. The joy of celebrating my own birthday was foreign to me, so in her room, decorated with flowers and candles, I stared in wonder when we were served a choice lunch ordered from the Imahan.

Her father, who doted upon her, arbitrarily declined all offers of marriage for his daughter when she came of age. And after her father's death, her mother, in turn, said no to all discussions of Shimeko-san's marriage. To the mother, who had served her domineering husband all her life, unable to talk back to him, her present life, alone with her daughter, was an easy one—one she would never willingly give up. She clung to her daughter and never loosened her grip until the end of her life.

After finishing the course in Girls' High School, Shimeko-san was an accountant for the same bank for thirty-seven years and in its subsidiary company the following ten years. She is still single and lives a quiet life together with a cousin in similar circumstances.

I looked at Shimeko-san before me again, appearing much younger than her age, with her face so full of life. I recalled the girl who used to wear a large ribbon in her hair and wondered where the power was hidden that enabled her to live on her own, with her back straight, as suits a courageous woman. I say this because, the question of her marriage aside, in her youth, Shimeko-san looked helpless, frail, and likely to be seduced by honeyed words. A man, rumored to be a philanderer, once said to me, "Asakusa women are difficult to court. They are not easily flattered." Indeed, many girls in Asakusa in those days refused to be flattered. Whatever others said about them, they scrutinized themselves with cool eyes and knew themselves.

When I was a fifth-grader, the music teacher decided that our class would perform an opera called *Momotaro* [The Peach Boy] for the school's Class Day, to which parents were invited. Shimeko-san's role was the dog, and mine was the pheasant. Because I was a poor singer, I was unhappy that I had been chosen. Shimeko-san whispered to me, "I think our teacher favors you and me. If we decline our parts, we will put her to shame. Then we would be unhappy." Smiling at each other, we did our best at rehearsals.

These views of Asakusa girls may suggest that, as children, we were without the charm of innocence. But we could not live properly without this pluck. When Asakusa girls left their parents against their wishes, acted against the norm of society, and experienced life's bitterness because of a man, their hearts burned with uncontrollable love—"uncontrollable," I say, because they knew beforehand that such bitterness would be the inevitable result of their act of love.

"The man I loved died in the war," Shimeko-san said as if looking far into the distance.

Shimeko-san said that not for a single moment did she think her work trying, even at her advanced age. But then she sighed for the first time and said, "These days, young girls are difficult to deal with." They act like pampered children, girls who cannot endure hardships without help. So they come to her when they are troubled and weep upon her breast. Yet in time, although Shimeko-san keeps their confidences to herself, they become distant because she knows their secrets.

Shimeko-san smiled quietly and sipped her hot, coarse tea with delight.

✦ ✦ ✦

The heartwarming chatter of two "old girls" has no end. Winter is near—time to warm ourselves before the fire.

The Girl from Akita[+]

 In the early summer of my first year of high school O-Yuki-san moved from Hokkaido to a house in a neighboring street. She left at the end of fall that year, so she was in Asakusa for less than six months. Yet I still remember her from time to time.

The man who brought her to our house for the first time was an old friend of my father and the most influ-

---

[+]Geography plays an important part in the conclusion of this essay. Akita is both a prefecture and the name of a city in the north of Honshu, the largest of the major islands that comprise Japan. Fukuoka is a city on the island of Kyushu, far to the south of Akita.

ential theatrical promoter in Hokkaido. My mother and I nicknamed this large, taciturn man Shoki-sama*, after the demon-destroyer of Chinese legend, whom he resembled, for he too wore a thick black beard covering his upper lip and chin. At the time, O-Yuki-san was twenty-two or twenty-three years old, I suppose. She was short with a full round face, and, though her nose was a little flat, her smooth skin was a transparent white. I had never seen such fine skin—soft and smooth, like white satin.

Shoki-sama had taken O-Yuki-san, who, it seems, was geisha in Akita, to Hokkaido and kept her as his mistress. But in less than three months, his wife had discovered the arrangement, which caused great trouble. After much fuss, Shoki-sama and O-Yuki-san separated—or so it seemed. Apparently, he had come to our home to obtain my father's help in that regard. Bowing as he made his request to Father, he said, "I want to keep O-Yuki in Tokyo, where I come once a month. Would you please take care of that for me?"

Behind Shoki-sama's stocky body, O-Yuki-san drooped her head as if she were bored. When I served them glasses of barley water, she came over to me—we had just met—with an expression of relief and spoke in the Akita dialect. When talking to me, she laughed, revealing beautiful white teeth, and spoke with a trill, as if the problems swirling around her only affected others. She showed no sign that her thoughts were troubled.

✦ ✦ ✦

Mother took to her immediately and found a cozy house for her nearby, saying, "She has all the charm of a cute little girl. No wonder men like her." To everybody's eyes, O-Yuki-san, who waited for Shoki-sama's monthly visit of a few days, seemed to be in an enviable position. My mother told the neighborhood women about her. And when they became acquainted with the newcomer, they were charmed by her modesty and cheerfulness. Even her heavy Akita dialect added to her appeal, and they called to her often in a friendly manner.

Occasionally, when Mother asked me, I cleaned O-Yuki-san's house because she was so poor at house-cleaning, laundry, and kitchen chores. She said to me, "I have no excuse to offer my master for living in luxury." She wouldn't hire a housekeeper, but instead tied cords on her slender shoulders to hold up her sleeves and tried to do the housework. When she saw O-Yuki-san's poor housekeeping skills, Mother sighed, "I can't look on without helping her. Perhaps she is so inept because since childhood, she was trained only in the arts of a geisha." However, these accomplishments were only mediocre. The *shamisen* music she occasionally played was average at best.

When I delivered the daily meal Mother prepared for her, O-Yuki-san said, "Asakusa is a lovely place. People from respectable households don't discriminate against a girl like me. I wish I could live here forever." She seemed happy, and as she spoke, tilted her head—her hair in the *marumage* style with a decorative pink chignon band. O-Yuki-san never said a word about her previous hard-ships or about her homelife as a child. Whenever some-one asked, she waved her white hands and said, "I've forgotten all that. My present life is a paradise—that's all that matters," and she laughed like a twittering bird. If she passed our house, she occasionally dropped in, but at home she idled away her time, lying on the *tatami* floor, skimming through issues of the magazine *Omoshiro Club* almost every day.

When summer had passed and the chilly autumn winds began to blow, a formal printed card arrived for my father from Hokkaido. It was from Shoki-sama's son, announcing that ten days earlier his father had died suddenly of a heart attack. Father rushed to O-Yuki-san with the card. Later, he said, she had gazed at it blankly for a long time. She had told him that Shoki-sama had come to Tokyo three weeks earlier and gone home in good spirits.

✦ ✦ ✦

At the beginning of November, O-Yuki-san decided to cancel the lease and return to Akita. The evening before her departure was damp with a cold rain falling. I took her a farewell gift from my mother. O-Yuki-san was lying with her head pillowed on her arm in the vacant room. She raised herself wearily. Her hair, done in the *sokuhatsu* style [a casual hairstyle, popular in Sawamura's youth] was in disorder. Her smiling face had lost its gloss, and her fair skin looked like paper. She said, "I appreciate what you have done for me during my stay here, O-Tei-chan."

I felt sorry for her and said, "Why don't you stay in Asakusa instead of going back to Akita?" But I knew she had no other choice.

"I really wish to stay, but I have no place to work. My accomplishments are not adequate for me to be a geisha here. I cannot do laundry, cooking, sewing, or anything else. Women like me have no means to live other than to depend on a man."

Suddenly, O-Yuki-san's usual smile had vanished. With tears rolling down her cheeks, she stared into my eyes and said, "But I don't want to depend on a man any more. O-Tei-chan, you are attending high school. Don't quit! Be firm and strong so that you won't have to rely on a man. A girl is human, too. She is not a dog to be sold and bought. I am through with that!" O-Yuki-san's fair hands covered her face, and she sobbed for some time. I felt that, for the first time, I had glimpsed the deepest recess of her heart. Not knowing how to console her, I, a young girl with no experience, also wept.

During the New Year season of the next year, a picture postcard offering season's greetings came from O-Yuki-san, who was to have returned to Akita. "I am doing well. I'll always remember Asakusa—Yuki." The message on the blank space of the card was written in a faltering hand. The card contained no sender's address, but it bore the postmark of Fukuoka, in Kyushu.

Tome-san's Lucky Direction

 Tome-san, the musical accompanist at the Miyato Theater, could often be found in the band section adjacent to the stage, beating a large drum, which caused his huge, protruding belly to vibrate. He had a fair complexion, small eyes, and shaggy, slanting eyebrows. And he always smiled. I liked Tome-san, but my younger brother, Tokunosuke, a child Kabuki actor, nicknamed him "Mr. Walkingsticks." Tome-san was just over forty, but his hairline had receded so that he was almost bald. He parted his hair on the side and painstakingly arranged the remaining hairs across the top of his head. These were as few as the walking sticks displayed at night stalls. That was the origin of his nickname.

Whatever happened to him, Tome-san never lost his composure or made a fuss, and his quiet demeanor and his ample proportions made him look every inch the prosperous master of a big shop. In fact, Tome-san was always completely broke and in desperate need of money. He was crazy about card games, yet he was a poor player and always lost.

In the beginning of December every year, Mr. Walkingsticks was the first to come to our house to pay the traditional year-end respect that employees at the theater paid to my father. In those days sugar was the customary year-end gift in Shitamachi. A bag of a few *kin* [about one-and-a-third pounds] of refined sugar was placed at the bottom of a large white bag, twelve by twenty inches, made of *washi* [traditionally made Japanese paper]. Such a cumbersome package was easily wrinkled and had to be carried carefully. That year Tome-san, wearing a worn-out cotton *haori* coat and a knit scarf, and burdened by his bulky body, carried the bag of sugar as if it were extremely delicate. He poked his head in at the kitchen door and spoke to me as I was washing rice. "Hi, Tei-bo. Working hard, are you?" he said. "Home?" he questioned, raising his right little finger, implying my mother.

"No, she's gone shopping in the neighborhood. But Father is home."

Bobbing his head, as if confused, he sighed thoughtfully. "I'll come again after doing some errands." Pulling himself together, he smiled and left. I knew why he was disappointed. If Mother were home, she would certainly give him a tip worth five times the sugar. Mother cut expenses for running the house, but she was always generous with others. My father took good care of others by giving them a job, but he would never give them a tip.

An hour later, when Tome-san stopped by our kitchen again, Mother was not back yet. He paused as if to say, "What shall I do?"

Just then my father appeared. "Oh, it's you, Tome-san. What's going on?"

Taken aback, Tome-san hid the bag of sugar behind his back and said, "Oh, nothing important. I'll come again."

"Oh, come on, Tome-san. Join us. Come on in," Father said.

Tome-san hesitated and said, "Well, I've just realized

that today your house lies in *ankensatsu*[+] from mine. I was unaware of that earlier. I'm sorry for my carelessness." As if his hulking body were shrinking, he scurried out, tripping on the board covering the ditch.

Father shook his head and said, "What a strange fellow! Well, let it be. I don't want to die anyway." Father laughed as he told me that *ankensatsu* was the worst direction in astrology; failing to avoid it would invite such a disaster as a servant killing his master.

In less than ten minutes, this dangerous Tome-san returned with Mother. They had met by chance on the main street. Adjusting the front of his kimono, which tended to come open because of his size, Tome-san sat properly on the wooden floor and offered a formal greeting: "I appreciate what you've done for me this year, Madam." The bag of sugar he presented after his polite greeting was rather crumpled.

As Tome-san was leaving, all smiles, I, a brash young girl, whispered to him from behind, "Isn't our house in your fatal direction?" He whispered in turn, "I made a tour of the neighborhood and *ankensatsu* has turned to *eho,* the lucky direction." He grinned, winking one of his small eyes. Mother's tip was probably very generous that year.

[+]*Ankensatsu* is considered the worst of the nine directions in astrology. This ominous direction changes from day to day and hour to hour.

An Imagawayaki[+] *and O-Teru-chan*

 It was the winter of my fourth year of high school. The rain that had started early that afternoon changed to sleet, and the biting cold of the night penetrated my skin. That year I was tutoring after school at a *hikitejaya** [a tea-house where men arranged to meet prostitutes], in the licensed quarters of Yoshiwara [the red-light district]. I was to prepare one of the owner's sons for the high school entrance examination. However, the boy had made little progress in his study. For the past three weeks, I had been struggling to interest him in arithmetic, his weakest subject.

The boy's room was in the back of the second floor. Naturally, in this house, the lively sounds of *shamisen* and drums drifted up from the front rooms. When that happened, the boy's eyes instantly lit up, and skillfully tapping the table with his pencil, he began to beat time to the music. After that, he was halfhearted in whatever I tried to teach. After one such session, I was fed up with my effort and his attitude.

At the time, the master of the house was one of my elder brother's patrons at the theater where he played young women's roles. This relationship continued to make me feel obliged to help his son. Yet I worried that I would have no excuse if the boy failed to pass the examination, while I had been receiving a generous

---

[+]The *imagawayaki* is a muffin named after the bridge, Imagawa, near the place where bean-jam muffins were first made.

monthly fee. So I thought that perhaps I should quit before that happened. This dilemma troubled me every day. Faced with this problem, I, the teacher, a seventeen-year-old high school girl, was at a loss and groaned under the weight of my responsibility.

That day, I taught until nearly ten at night and then left by the back door. I picked my way along the muddy road, trudging in my rain clogs. The pattering of the rain on my old umbrella with a bull's-eye design sounded dreary. To make matters worse, I had had a slight cold for two or three days. Though wearing a quilted *haori* jacket I felt a chill in my shoulders. I pulled my woolen shawl tight and, going by way of the Ryusen-ji temple, turned the corner of the street into Umamichi.

Just then the *koshidaka shoji* door [a sliding paper screen with a wooden base for protection] of an *imagawayaki* shop before me slid open. Before me, I heard a familiar clear and high-pitched voice saying, "Well, I'll come again. Good night." Without thinking, I said, "O-Teru-chan, is that you?" Taken by surprise, she stared into the darkness and then ran under my umbrella. "Where have you been at this late hour?" she said. "You look so blue!"

O-Teru-chan and I were friends in a *nagauta* [a type of singing] music class, and she was one year my senior. She had a natural aptitude for the *nagauta* and was studying hard to eventually teach it. We rarely saw each other after I had entered high school, but in our primary school days, we were always together. As a result, we were nicknamed *omiki-dokkuri,* because we were like the pair of saké bottles offered before the temple altar.

That night, she and her friends had been practicing

nagauta until late and had drawn lots at the Amida* lottery. With money they had collected, O-Teru-chan had come to the shop to buy *imagawayaki* for the group. From O-Teru-chan's pockets floated the aroma of *imagawayaki* hot from the pan, and it tempted me to buy some to take home. While waiting for my muffins to be baked, O-Teru-san said that the moment she saw me, she noticed my glum expression and that she was concerned. As she listened to my story of the *shamisen*-loving boy I was tutoring who had made no progress in his study and who was driving me to my wit's end, she laughed cheerfully as always and said, "Don't worry if he fails. It's not your fault. He must like *shamisen* better than his studies, just like me. He should become a *shamisen* teacher, shouldn't he? It's foolish to think that every boy should go to high school. It's okay for you, though, because you are more fond of studying than of gaining artistic skills."

O-Teru-chan's words comforted me, and I felt my burden eased somewhat. After promising to meet in the New Year season for a long chat, we parted. As I began walking toward Saruwaka-machi, the sleet had already changed to snow. The package of the just-baked *imagawayaki* warmed me. I felt that, before I had realized it, O-Teru-chan had grown much more mature than I. At the end of that month, I quit tutoring the boy.

Forty-odd years have gone by, and the boy has become an excellent *nagauta* teacher. What became of O-Teru-chan, I do not know. Even now, when I pass an *imagawayaki* shop, I am seized by a longing to see her.

Children Are Creatures of the Outdoors

 I finished putting away our summer clothing and exchanging it for our winter clothing. The final garment I took from the clothes chest was a *dotera* [a quilted dressing gown]. I found tacking threads still in it. Oh, yes, I remembered. I had re-sewn it but never worn it. Judging from my past, in the spring I may end up putting it away again without wearing it.

Come to think of it, I rarely see people wearing quilted clothing these days. In my childhood, when December arrived, we were thickly clad in kimono, haori jackets, and *chanchanko* [sleeveless jackets], all quilted with cotton. Even wearing all this clothing, when we were outdoors, we were cold; our cheeks and the tips of our noses turned very red.

The only heat in our schoolroom was a potbelly coal stove. I remember our teacher once scolded us for gabbing around it until the embers turned to ashes. When winter came, Shitamachi residents made a charcoal fire in an oblong *hibachi,* and every household kept an iron kettle singing all day. Yet every time a *fusuma* [a sliding partition made of thick paper] or a *shoji* [a sliding framed door with thin paper panels that admit light] was opened, cold wind entered.

The only warmth that children had was an *anka* [a foot-warmer, a small earthen vessel containing hot coals]. A blanket and *futon* [a thick quilt], which covered the *anka,* were slightly warm, and putting our cold soles directly on the even warmer *anka* felt so cozy and comfortable. If we continued to warm ourselves too long, our mothers drove us out, saying "Why don't you go outdoors and play? Look how you're behaving. You aren't retired old men, are you? Remember, children are creatures of the outdoors." Recklessly, we gathered our courage and ran out into the snow—barefoot! In its own way, playing like that was fun, and we romped like puppies.

Strangely enough, although we wore quilted clothing both indoors and outdoors, we wore no socks. It was not because we had no *tabi* [socks with a separate space for the big toe to fit into clogs], for I remember Mother forced us to wear *tabi* socks with our best New Year's outfits. But at other times we didn't wear them. I believe it was much later, when I was no longer a child, that I regularly wore colored velveteen *tabi* socks.

Only children from wealthy houses wore gloves. But we looked like *yakko-dako* [kites shaped like stylish footmen with hands covered by their sleeves], with our cold, numb hands pulled into our tight sleeves. Or we secretly inserted our hands into the openings of our kimono at the armpits and held them to our chests. If our parents caught us doing that, they scolded us for our bad manners. But many children held their hands to their chests, in part, because they were ashamed to have frostbitten fingers, which were red and thick. Yet sometimes a boy would boast to his friends of his frostbitten hands, saying, "Look at my hands. Aren't they great?" Then he would triumphantly scratch his hands that had warmed and become itchy. Another would suddenly shout out: "Oh, no! My hands are more swollen than yours." On such occasions I, whose hands were only chapped, not frostbitten, felt ashamed.

Children are creatures of the outdoors. Compared with children today, who watch television in a centrally heated house, those who romped about in the cold, with bare hands and feet, thickly clad in quilted clothing, were more healthy—both in mind and body.

But in those days, few cars were on the streets, so they were safe—although very muddy.

The Night of the Hagoita[+] *Fair*

 Aunt O-Seki had been a geisha in Yoshiwara in both her young and in her mature years. She was my mother's aunt and was already well over sixty when I was a child. But if I called her Granny [Obaa-san] by mistake, she would retort crisply: "No Grannying me, thank you! I am not yet senile enough to be called Granny." Although her face was wrinkled, Aunt O-Seki's shapely nose, large eyes, and slender figure suggested refinement. My father said, "She was once a beauty and has seen better days." Child though I was, his comment convinced me. She

---

[+]*Hagoita* fairs are held throughout Japan in December. The one at Senso-ji temple takes place December 17–19. A *hagoita* is a long, rectangular paddle used in a game with shuttlecocks. Those described here are for purely decorative purposes.

236 ◆ *My Asakusa*

was the best *shamisen* player in Yoshiwara. Because she was high spirited, Aunt O-Seki was compared to a geisha with a similar temperament and ability, Yakko-no-Koman, and because she practiced her trade in Yoshiwara, which was surrounded by a *hori* [moat], my aunt was referred to by the laudatory nickname Hori-no-Koman.*

Aunt O-Seki quit being a geisha while still in her prime at age thirty-five or thirty-six because she broke her right wrist and was unable to play the *shamisen*. When I was old enough to remember, she lived in a *nagaya* [a row house apartment for low-income people] behind the Asakusa Primary School. She lived meagerly, supported only by her adopted daughter's income from sewing. When I was a child, my aunt seemed to be a grumpy, nagging old lady.

In December of my ninth year of *kazoe**, my father and older brother Tomokazu went to Kyushu on a provincial tour with his company, and, as ill luck would have it, at the same time, my younger brother Toku-nosuke had to go to Hokuriku on a similar tour. Mother had to accompany him. So I would have been left to attend to the house. Rejecting that option, Mother asked Aunt O-Seki to look after the house during her absence. "Don't worry. Leave it to me," she said and, thumping her chest, saw them off.

I was soon to learn what Aunt O-Seki meant by "leave it to me." Each day, she left all chores—cooking, laundry, as well as cleaning—to me, a mere child. Her disabled hand had to be considered, but she was as glib as ever. Whenever she opened her mouth, she made comments such as, "A first-rate geisha was never trained in such contemptible tasks as kitchen work." With her nose in the air and seated in the place of the master in front of the *nagahibachi** [an oblong, charcoal-burning heater], she spent all day smoking—using her left hand.

On December 18, the day of *Hagoita* Fair, Aunt O-Seki said after dinner, "Why don't we go to the fair? I haven't been there for a long time." I cheerfully agreed to her exceptionally kind proposal. Stalls made of thick, round timber frames with hanging straw partitions lined the street from the Niō Gate to the back of the main temple. They sold *hagoita* with collages from *Dojoji* and *Sukeroku* [two Kabuki plays] beautifully made with red, blue, purple, gold, and silver silk cloth. Young men with thin cotton towels rolled into head-bands and tied around their foreheads were shouting vigorously to attract customers.

Perhaps because it was the first of its kind that season [of the many *Hagoita* fairs annually held in Tokyo, Asakusa's was the first], Asakusa's Hagoita-ichi was as crowded as if all the people of Tokyo had flocked together. Among the paying customers were girls just window-shopping and frequently squealing joyously at the likenesses of their favorite actors on the paddles. It was an exhilarating and charming scene.

At one point, my aunt said to me, "Look, Tei-bo. That *hagoita* over there has a picture on it of *O-Yoshi the Boa: The Courtesan of Yoshiwara* [the title and central character of a Kabuki play]." Aunt O-Seki forcibly elbowed her way through the girls in front of her to reach the big paddle. But she lost her balance, swayed momentarily, and almost fell. The young vendor quickly grasped her in his arms and said, "Be careful, lady. I'm afraid you have no chance of winning even if you compete with young girls." Hearing the girls' giggles, my aunt's face became stern, and she shook herself free of the young man.

Just then, a commotion arose among the crowd a little further ahead of us. We heard a woman shout, "Look! Here comes Utaemon [a Kabuki actor, famous for his portrayal of females]. He's so handsome, isn't he?" In front of the crowd that quickly made way for him, I saw the face of one of the most popular actors of the time. He had on none of the traditional makeup and was wearing a gray Western overcoat with a cape and gold-rimmed, pale blue spectacles. He slowly walked past us, with young geisha clinging to him. Aunt O-Seki said abruptly, "Let's go home," and walked quickly, urging me to hurry. She didn't even glance back.

That evening my aunt sent me to buy some *saké*. A cup or two of cold *saké* quickly intoxicated her. Her age showed after all. Then she said, "The times are out of joint. Look at those geisha who followed Narikomaya [Utaemon's hereditary stage title]. The way they did their hair and dressed was not up to the mark at all. To call themselves geisha! I'm simply flabbergasted. I bet they are pillow geisha [geisha who practice prostitution]."

Yoshiwara geisha did not sleep with their guests. My great-aunt, Hori-no-Koman, had been completely independent, with nobody to fear, and practiced her trade only with her *shamisen*. She never followed an actor about; rather, actors followed her. Many men about town frequented Yoshiwara in hopes of seeing her rather than an *oiran* [a prostitute of high rank]. The old woman who had lost the use of her hand and sat grumbling to a child in the middle of the night was a dreary and pitiful sight, even to me.

The injury to her right hand, which held the plectrum for the *shamisen*—the hand more precious to her than her own life—was caused by a fall from a *rikisha* on her way back from her New Year's visit to the Kawasaki Daishi Temple. I had heard her tell of the accident often: "The *rikisha* man tripped on a stone, and the cart toppled over sideways. Because of that silly old man, whose services I had used for many years . . ." Her wristbone had been horribly broken, and, when the bandage was removed a few months later, the bone had set in an inwardly crooked and disfigured way. The accident had happened a long time ago when the state of medical science . . . In short, the surgery for which she paid her entire fortune was unsuccessful.

Aunt O-Seki had reached the pinnacle of her career as a geisha and in her best days had had everything her own way: no patron, no husband, no fear of poverty (she had complete confidence that she could always earn money giving *shamisen* lessons)—complete independence. After the accident, she was deprived of the means to display the art which she had polished for so many years. What a pity! As she drank her *saké,* Aunt O-Seki spoke of her past independence: "Until my injury, I used to go to the fair every year and never failed to buy the most expensive *hagoita,* one three-foot long. All the young vendors who saw me begged for my patronage. I wish I had died when my hand was injured and put an end to it." So saying, Aunt O-Seki emptied her cup with one gulp and was silent for some time. Then she sighed and continued her lament: "However, I believe I am more fortunate than your mother, Tei-bo. She has been a drudge in the kitchen all her life. In spite of my bad luck, at one time I earned money, spent it, and did what I liked. I have seen better days—I lived like a man!" As she spoke, tears streaked her wrinkled cheek, and a faint smile appeared on her face. I didn't know what to say. I just nodded for no reason.

The old wall clock ticked away. It sounded exceptionally loud.

Mattress-Making

With a towel wrapped around her head and her sleeves held up with a cord, Mother began to cover the cabinets and her dresser with large wrappers with a *karakusa* design [a vine leaf pattern]. Ah, I thought, today we will quilt our bedding with cotton. This made my heart sink a little. "Come on," Mother coaxed, "Give me a hand. Hurry up, or the day will be over before we're finished." I retied my apron and covered my head with a towel.

In Shitamachi in those days, families rarely bought ready-made bedding. Making mattresses was one of a housewife's routine chores in early winter. And when I was a girl, Mother made certain I learned to do it properly: "A little more cotton must be stuffed than the size of the cloth suggests; otherwise, lumps of cotton will shift about in the bedding. Corners must be sewn tight. Look, you've got a cake-like mass of cotton formed there." Mother seemed to have much confidence in her skills in making bedding, and she was quite particular about how to do it.

In the light, fluffy dust of rising cotton, Mother worked briskly, while I stood idle, confused and unable to be of much help among the bedding, which was spread throughout our small room. We enjoyed seeing the washed and stretched cloth that we had finished sewing the night before turning into comfortable, warm bedding, and its soft texture touch was a pleasure too.

Particularly difficult to make was a *kaimaki* [worn for additional warmth beneath the bed coverings]. These days, we rarely see a *kaimaki*, but it is like a *dotera* [a dressing gown] made of a very thick material and amply quilted with cotton. In those days, with nothing but an *anka* [an earthen foot warmer] to warm our cold hands and feet, a *kaimaki* was indispensable protection in every household against the cold. Its puffy, well-stuffed sleeves covered the sleeper's cold shoulders, and the black velvet neck bands protected the neck and chin from a cold draft. The comforting warmth of a *kaimaki* lives with me still.

I recall the early winter of my sixteenth or seventeenth year, and Mother was full of pep, saying she was going to replace the cotton in all the family mattresses. I worked hard helping her with this undertaking from early morning. Toward evening, when we had almost finished stuffing the cotton and were having tea, when we heard a voice at the lattice door of our house. There, a woman, sixty-four or sixty-five years old, was standing before us, carrying a large bundle in a wrapper. It looked as though her lean body would break under the burden. She said to Mother, "Excuse me. I wonder if you would kindly help an old woman?"

Always ready to help someone, Mother said, "Oh dear! Just come in. You must rest." Mother helped the woman lower her bundle on the entrance step and offered her a cup of freshly made hot tea. In the old woman's bundle was a mattress that she wanted to sell. Compared to the mattresses we made, the cloth and pattern of the woman's mattress were inferior, and the cotton seemed mediocre at best. Mother asked her the price. When the old woman told us, Mother and I exchanged glances. In the end, Mother loosened her purse strings after all.

The old woman folded her wrapper and placed it under her *obi* sash and thanked Mother many times. After the woman left, Mother looked embarrassed and in defense of her action told me what the woman had said: "She says her daughter-in-law gives her no spending money, so she made the mattresses and came all the way from Chiba to sell them. She went from door to door but was able to sell only one. And now it's almost evening." Listening to my tenderhearted mother's excuse, I comforted her: "Well, it can't be helped. You could have done little else."

Just then, the grocer's wife appeared at our kitchen door and said, "Hello. I was wondering if I could ask a favor of you?" She was carrying a new mattress under her arm. After telling of a similar meeting with the woman who had just left us, our neighbor said, "Well, she was an old woman, so I bought the mattress out of pity in spite of myself. When my husband came home and learned about it, he was furious at what I had done. I am quite at a loss. Do you think you could afford to buy another mattress?" As an answer, Mother silently showed her the thin mattress she had just bought. "Oh my!" she responded. Gazing at each other, the two impulsive women burst out laughing.

Then, as if shaking off something, Mother tucked up her sleeves again and said, "Now we must finish the mattresses. Get me the sewing kit, O-Tei." The grocer's wife shrugged her shoulders and left, neglecting to close the door. A cold wind blew through our house.

Crazy About Acting

 Toku-chan, "Mr. Come, Come Now," has suddenly passed away. On July 30, the fiftieth year of Showa [1975]. Age sixty four. Died of colon cancer. Name: Tokunosuke Kato. Stage name: Daisuke Kato. He was my younger brother. Gentle by nature, Tokunosuke disliked conflicts of any sort. If any dissension arose among people around him, he would say,"Come, come now," pat the disputing parties on the shoulder with his large, thick hands, and try to settle the disagreement. Now his good-natured, round face can be seen no longer.

Born and bred in Asakusa, fathered by a Kabuki stage director whose dream was to make all his children actors, and following his brother Kunitaro Sawamura, Tokunosuke made his stage debut at the Miyato Theater at the age of five by *kazoe**. Was he a born actor? I wonder. Playing the roles of Sankichi in *Shigenoi Parting from Her Child;* Senmatsu in *Sendaihagi: The Story of a Household Disturbance of the Daté Clan;* and Otsuru in *Maelstrom of Awa,* Tokunosuke was immediately identified with his character and moved theater-lovers to tears. He was praised as a first-rate child actor.

My little brother caused quite a stir when, at the request of Master Sojuro Sawamura the Seventh, he played Ishidomaru in *Karukaya* at the Imperial Theater. My father was thrilled, saying that a child actor from a small theater, who was not part of an established family of actors, had enthralled the audience at one of the top theaters in the country. But such praise did not impress my brother very much. He was happy as long as he could act on the stage, whether at the Imperial Theater or at the Miyato. "I'll be a fine actor when I grow up, and I'll see that you have your favorite fruit every day, so don't cry, Sister," he used to say whenever I, who was his attendant at the theater, became frustrated with him.

You see, once offstage, Tokunosuke was an incorrigibly mischievous boy. As time passed, and fewer and fewer appropriate roles allowed him to appear on the stage—the stage he loved so much—this naughty boy grew into a gentle man who endured almost all difficulties with patience.

The life of a child actor is very short. After age ten, cuteness, his essential quality, is lost. "Everybody passes through this difficult halfway period," people said, hoping to soothe and comfort Tokunosuke. In the meantime, he resigned himself to continue his schooling, but

I could plainly see that he was impatient to be on the stage again.

When he finally completed middle school [the equivalent of high school] and started serious training as an actor with the Kabuki-za Troupe, my brother realized how high the wall of his origin was in blocking his way. His appearance at the Imperial Theater as Ishidomaru was an exception, overlooked because he played a child actor's role.

In those days, in the world of Kabuki, players who were not from an established acting family had no chance of success, however hard they struggled. The roles occasionally given to them were those for "other characters," the minor characters who spoke only a few words once the curtain rose. Our elder brother, Kunitaro Sawamura, a handsome young player of female parts, left the world of Kabuki to become a movie actor simply because the wall denied him access. Unlike the usual leading man, Tokunosuke had the features of a character actor—a bony, solid build with a dark, round face. Without a handsome appearance to help him, all he could do was work backstage wearing the traditional black clothing and gaze enviously at the actors from illustrious families.

When he devoted himself to learning to dance, Tokunosuke's remarkable progress astonished his teacher, but making a living as a dancer was far from his intention. If he could dance well, he might be given parts in *shosagoto* [scenes in a Kabuki play where dance alone communicates the meaning], where this skill, rather than his appearance, would earn him the better roles. That was his hope, but the best he ever got was the minor role of Karami-no-Hanayoten* [a foil to the lead

246 ◆ *My Asakusa*

actor]. "I am going to quit the stage, Sister," he once said during this period, gripping my hand and shedding tears of bitter frustration. It was a pitiful sight.

Mother looked at him lovingly and said, "I am sorry that you were not born with better looks. But if you train yourself and become an excellent actor, you will succeed some day even though you are neither handsome nor wellborn. I am sure you will." Mother protected her son from all hardships except those related to the stage. She used to tell him not to worry and to concentrate on the stage—to "work like crazy to become a good actor."

Mother's loving care was taken over wholly by Tokunosuke's wife, Masako. She was born in Asakusa, too. When she married my brother, this former star of the Shochiku Girls Operetta Troupe quit that magnificent stage without hesitation. She always stood close behind him, like a shadow, and dealt with all troublesome and unpleasant matters that might bother him.

When asked what he liked best, Brother's immediate answer was, "First, the stage, second, the stage, and third—the stage again." He was crazy about acting. This totally dedicated actor, Daisuke Kato, grew into a modest, guileless man, protected by two generations of Asakusa women, my mother and his wife. He was simply an actor and retained his boyish innocence. His favorites were simple foods—bean-jam buns, strawberries, and tuna *sushi*.

Tokunosuke joined the Zenshin-za Company and threw himself into theater life, but he was then drafted for military service in World War II. He was sent to New Guinea, and as leader of the Entertainment Squad, was fortunate to be able to present plays there—an assignment he never expected. Many soldiers in New Guinea were wounded or killed in air raids or died from starvation. One can only imagine how much they enjoyed the plays presented in the middle of the jungle at the hurriedly built "Manokwari Kabuki Theater."

Tokunosuke's wig was made from the tail of a horse, and he danced to a *shamisen* made of tin. I believe he treasured the joy of acting every day. The particulars of this aspect of his life appear in his book *Snow Falls on the Island in the South*. Former members of the Entertainment Squad later told me, "Squad Leader Kato was usually a very gentle and kind man. But in rehearsing a play, he was a tyrant. We feared him." Luckily, my brother survived and came home.

After the war, he took special care of his health. He used to say, "Health is an actor's capital, you know." Ever since his youth, Tokunosuke had shown no interest in drinking, smoking, gambling, or affairs with women. He was not interested in luxury nor did he cause anyone trouble. He spent his time improving his skills as an actor. His only form of relaxation was to be at home, together with his dear wife and child. He was such a serious-minded actor that his life was, like a good movie, worthy, as we say, "to be recommended by the Ministry of Education."

After a starring role in the Toho company's movie *Oban*, Brother's late-blooming flowers were about to bear fruit in television and on the stage. I'm sad to say that at precisely this time, Tokunosuke suddenly passed away. His death was the most serious blunder for an actor of his caliber. And I am angry about it. He ignored the priority of age—I am his elder sister!

Our sole consolation was that Brother remained

ignorant of the nature of his disease until the last moment. For several months his son, his only child and his pride, kept to himself the doctor's dreadful pronouncement—"Daisuke Kato will never appear on the stage again." The son was fully aware of how great a blow this knowledge would be to his father.

Believing his illness was a liver disorder, Tokonosuke was content with his wife's constant bedside nursing. Once when I visited him he said to me, "I have not been ill thus far in my life, so I guess I can't complain that I may be long in recovering from my present illness. But I am lucky, Sister, to have a very good nurse." Then he said, "I saw Mother in a dream last night. I told her I had a stomachache, and she said, 'Now don't you worry. Masako is with you.' Mother knows best, doesn't she?" While he stroked his worn and thin neck, his eyes, like those of a spoiled child, followed his wife, who was grating an apple for him.

I recall him telling me of his hope for his future: "I wish to get well soon and appear in a good play. This time I'm sure I'll be a better actor, an actor who performs with a quiet and refined charm, like that of antique silver. I feel that, at long last, I have grasped the essence. Just you wait and see, Sister." Tokunosuke did not doubt that, in the following year at the latest, he would return to the stage. I had no choice but to put on a bright face and nod in agreement. That was very painful.

Until the end, Brother also retained his desire to help others: "An actor must have good basics, mustn't he? I want to hand down to young actors what I have learned. In New Guinea, I gave vocal exercises to soldiers, complete amateurs who eked out an existence by eating potato leaves. Thanks to this elementary training, we managed to present plays that entertained seven thousand men. I heard of a squad leader who yelled into the ear of one soldier dying from malnutrition, 'Pull yourself together. Tomorrow is our unit's theater day. Are you going to die before you see it?'" Hearing this, my brother said, the soldier came to life again.

As my brother talked bit by bit about his New Guinea days, his sunken cheeks gained some color, and he looked happy. Just as the Entertainment Squad was enjoying increasing popularity, the commander was summoned home for promotion. The Lieutenant General, who had been impressed by Brother's plays, wanted to take Tokunosuke with him to his new assignment. It was a golden opportunity to return home alive, but, after painful deliberation, Brother declined. His explanation was typical of him: "I dared not go home and leave the audiences who enjoyed our plays so much." For nearly four years until the war was over, Tokunosuke continued to present plays in the jungles of New Guinea, literally at the risk of his life.

After his repatriation, Brother called on the playwright Shin Hasegawa to apologize for staging his plays without first obtaining permission. The playwright said, "I envy you as an actor. Few performances have been so thoroughly enjoyed. An actor's talent lies in pleasing his audience." Hasegawa-san's words encouraged Brother to strive even harder. Recalling the incident, Brother said to me, "So, Sister, I wish to be a better actor and have my audiences enjoy my performances."

✦ ✦ ✦

While in the hospital, Brother managed to appear in the TV drama *Six Seagulls,* which was to be his last role. When his performance was being videotaped, he was still concerned with the nuances of acting. Turning to his son, who was gently supporting him from behind, he said, "Do you think something is wrong with the way I am smoking? Somehow it doesn't seem right." My nephew was unable to answer and looked away, he told me, for the doctor had informed him that his father had no hope of recovery.

This good-hearted actor, looked after with loving care by two women, his mother and his wife, this modest man who never lost the integrity he showed as a novice, was suddenly snatched away by cancer. Oh, how I hate that disease!

✦ *Glossary* ✦

THIS IS NOT AN EXHAUSTIVE LIST OF THE JAPANESE terms used in the text. The purpose of the Glossary is to provide further information and to avoid repeating the explanation each time the term appears. When a brief clarification, inserted after the Japanese between commas, brackets, or parentheses, is sufficient and if the phrase does not appear often elsewhere, it is not included in the Glossary. The terms included here are marked with asterisks in the text. When the word appears often, such as with *shamisen, haori,* or *hakama,* no asterisk is used on the assumption that the term is already familiar. When a Japanese word appears for the first time, the reader can obtain the necessary information without consulting the Glossary and thereby interrupting the reading. For example, "*tabi* sock" indicates that *tabi* is a type of sock worn on the foot. When certain information is required for understanding an essay, that explanation is placed in a footnote at the beginning of the essay and omitted from the Glossary, as in the cases of "My First Day at Asakusa Primary School," "My Burgeoning Curiosity," "Mother and the *Shobu* Bath" and "Otori-sama: The Festival of the Rooster." We hope that with these devices the reader can enjoy the essays without much interruption.

In writing parts of this Glossary, we owe much to *Japan, An Illustrated Encyclopedia* (JIE), Edwin O. Reischauer, Ichiro Kato, et. al., eds., (Tokyo: Kodansha, 1993). In each of the eight cases, we acknowledge our debt.

– A –

Address, forms of
"-sama" is the most polite suffix added to the name of a
person addressed or referred to. Hence, it is also used in
referring to a god, such as Awashima-sama, Otori-sama,
Konnichi-sama.
"-san" is an honorific used between adults.
"-bo" is a suffix of endearment used by an adult to a child,
usually a boy.
"-chan" is also a suffix of endearment used by an adult in
addressing a child or between children addresssing each
other.

ame   A sticky substance made of starch sugared by malt

Amida lottery   Radiating lines are drawn on a piece of white
paper. At the concealed ends, a different sum of money is
written on each line. Participants write their names at the
open ends of the lines of their choice. When the concealed
ends are revealed, the participants contribute the amounts
written on their lines. The collected sum purchases refresh-
ments which are divided equally. The lottery is called Amida
(Amitabha) because the lines look like radiating shafts of
Amitabha's halo.

anka   A clay foot warmer (see "kotatsu")

ankensatsu   An evil direction, not fixed but changing from day
to day and hour to hour

Asama-gongen   A god dwelling on Mount Fuji and widely wor-
shiped in Japan. The shrine dedicated to Asama-gongen at
Kisakata-machi (also known as O-Fuji-sama) is frequented by
Asakusa area worshipers, who receive the same blessing as do
the pilgrims climbing Mount Fuji.

Azuma school of the two-stringed koto   The Azuma school, initiated by Rosen Tosha, developed from the original school begun by Nakayama and Kuzuhara in 1820. The initiator's name is inherited by succeeding masters.

– B –

-bo   See "Address, forms of."

Bon Festival   August 13–16 (new calendar), when ancestral spirits are believed to return to their homes in this world. In Tokyo the Bon is observed in July.

Boys' Festival   Called the Tango Festival or Iris Festival, it is held on May 5. Carp streamers are flown outside the house, warrior dolls are displayed, and *chimaki* [rice cake wrapped in cogon grass or bamboo leaves] and *kashiwamochi* [rice cakes filled with sweet bean paste and wrapped in oak leaves] are eaten. In China it was customary to hang mugwort from the eaves of the roof to repel disease. Since sweet flag [*shobu* or iris] was believed to have the same effect, a combination of sweet flag and mugwort became the practice.

bream   An expensive fish eaten on an auspicious occasion

brown algae   A seaweed, growing on the rocks of rough, shallow beaches, and harvested while young. When dried, it is black and is often eaten with fried bean curd which has been cooked with soy sauce and sugar.

Bunraku   Puppetry with *joruri* chanting of a dramatic text. Puppets are about one-half to two-thirds life-size. The term "bunraku" is derived from Bunraku-za, a puppet theater organized in the Kansei Period (1789–1800) by Bunrakuken Uemura in Osaka.

– C –

-chan See "Address, forms of."

chikuwa Fish paste in the shape of a thick stick, two-thirds of
a foot long, with a hole in it

– D –

Daikoku The god of wealth, one of the Seven Deities of Good
Fortune

Doll's Festival (Hina-matsuri) Festival for girls held on March
3. Dolls in ancient court dress, representing the emperor and
empress, attendants, and musicians, are placed on tiered platforms. Children eat *hishimochi* [diamond-shaped rice cakes]
and drink *shirozake* [made from rice malt and *saké*].

– E –

Edokko A person born and bred in Edo (currently Tokyo), but
strictly speaking, the third generation of those so born. Work-
ing-class people in the early nineteenth century began to
boast of being the citizens of Edo, the Shogunate's seat, but
from about 1750, longtime Edo residents developed a sense
of unity and pride around their studious nonchalance about
adhering to the aesthetic canon of *iki* [chic] or stylishness,
and other personal qualities such as chivalry, frankness, crisp
speech, openheartedness, and liberality with money. At the
same time, they could be imprudent, hot-tempered, vain,
stubborn, and exclusive. "Edokko" is still applied today to
Tokyoites with these characteristics.

– F –

Fujimusume A dance in a Kabuki play, in which a girl holding a festoon of wisteria flowers dances to *nagauta* music

fusuma A sliding door, a series of which serves as a partition between adjacent rooms

futon A thick mattress and bed quilt, usually padded with cotton

– G –

geisha A female entertainer who provides companionship. When she has acquired the most important skills in the repertoire—conversation, playing the shamisen, singing, and dancing—a geisha can have a career even after her youth and beauty have faded. Geisha are registered in the geisha union of the area, receive their assignments through the *kemban* (registry office), and entertain their guests in a restaurant which is a member of the restaurant union.

A geisha's relations with men may be of several types. A geisha tries to develop a clientele of dependable favorite customers *[gohiiki]*. Although it is now possible to make a living from wages and tips, before World War II, a geisha generally had a patron *[dan'na]*, with whom she was involved emotionally, sexually, and economically. Occasionally a geisha marries a customer and leaves the profession.

Children were often adopted into geisha houses *[okiya]* for training, and sometimes they were indentured there by their parents. As part of their discipline, these girls (called *shikomi*) were assigned much of the household drudgery. Apprentice geisha, thirteen to eighteen years old, are called *oshaku* and *hangyoku* [half-jewel] in the Kanto area and *maiko* in the Kansai region. Before she attains full geisha status, an apprentice undergoes the "deflowering ceremony" *[mizuage]* with some important customer. *(Adapted from JIE)*

– H –

hagoita A wooden paddle in the game *hanetsuki,* a girls' game for one or two and played at the New Year's holidays. Developed in the fifteenth century, the game is still played today. A *hagoita* fair is held in December. A *hagoita* is used with a *hane* (shuttlecock) made of soapberry seed and feathers. When two people play, the game resembles badminton without a net. On the front side of the *hagoita* is a picture of such auspicious symbols as pine, bamboo, or plum trees, or portraits of beautiful women. During the Edo period, the decorations on the *hagoita* became increasingly elaborate, and the figures of popular Kabuki actors were often made of silk collage.

hakama A formal skirt

han'eri A replaceable neckpiece

haori A formal half coat, often worn with a *hakama*

haragake A waistcoat having a front but no back, worn by a workman

hikitejaya A teahouse in the licensed quarters where a guest requested a certain prostitute and paid for all services before being taken to her home; formerly called *ageya*

hittsume Hair drawn back into a bun

Hori-no-Koman A moat *(hori)* surrounded the Yoshiwara licensed quarters to prevent girls from escaping. This nickname was probably given to Sawamura-san's aunt, who was a Yoshiwara geisha and was as spirited as Yakko-no-Koman. See "Yakko-no-Koman."

Hotei   A god with a potbelly, one of the Seven Deities of Good Fortune

hozuki   The ground cherry or Chinese lantern plant. The lantern-shaped pod bears a cherry-like fruit, which is kneaded carefully until soft and the pulp and seeds removed through a small hole. Young girls press the empty skin between the tongue and the palate to produce squeaking sounds. Imitations of this toy are made from the egg pouches of a shellfish known as whelk, similar in shape to the fruit. In Japanese these imitations are called *umi* [sea] *hozuki* and *naginata* [halbert] *hozuki* (shaped like a halbert blade). Manufactured versions are made of rubber or other materials. The Hozuki Fair is held at the Senso-ji temple on July 10. *(Adapted from JIE)*

– I –

imagawayaki   Muffin containing bean jam, served hot

Inari   The god of harvests

– J –

jikkan   Literally, "ten trunks." When years are named, *junishi* is combined with jikkan, resulting in sixty different combinations, forming a sixty-year cycle. One celebrates the sixtieth year of life, *kanreki,* meaning one has lived one whole cycle. *Jikkan* are wood, fire, earth, metal, water, each combined with *e* (elder brother) and *to* (younger brother), or *ko, otsu, hei, tei, bo, ki, kou, shin, jin,* and *ki. (Adapted from JIE)*

joruri   Narrative chanting accompanied by the shamisen in Bunraku puppet theater

junishi   Literally, "twelve branches." An ancient system, originally Chinese, for counting days, months, and years, but also used to indicate directions and the divisions of the day. The twelve branches came to be represented as animals: rat, ox, tiger, hare, dragon, snake, horse, sheep, monkey, rooster, dog, and boar. Because a month is usually thirty or thirty-one days, some days of the twelve branches occur only twice, and some three times. *(Adapted from JIE)*

– K –

Kabuki   The traditional Japanese play which flourished in the Edo period (1603–1868) and is still performed. Plays are set in the Edo or previous periods and are accompanied by music of the three-stringed shamisen, drums, and singing. All roles, male and female, are performed by male actors.

kamishimo   In the Edo period, a warrior's ceremonial dress, worn with a *hakama*

Kannon   The goddess of mercy

Kantei   A calligrapher of the late Edo period, whose style still graces the signs, brochures, and other advertising of the Kabuki theater

Karami-no-Hanayoten   *Hanayoten* is the costume, therefore the role, of a soldier or raiding constable. *Karami* (literally, "becoming entangled") is the foil who sets off the leading actor in a stage fight. Hence, *Karami-no-Hanayoten* is a subordinate officer trying, without success, to capture a hero/culprit.

Kawanakajima   Located between the Rivers Chikuma and Sai in Nagano, where a series of engagements (1553–1564) was fought between Uesugi Kenshin of Echigo and Takeda Shingen of Kai. The battles became a theme in *joruri* and Kabuki.

Kawasaki Daishi   A popular temple in the city of Kawasaki, in which the image of Kobo Daishi, the founder of the Shingon sect of Buddhism, is housed. The image is thought to ward off evils.

kazoe-doshi   One's age counted in the old way (see page 79)

Kikugoro Onoe the Sixth   Onoe Kikugoro is a distinguished hereditary name of Kabuki actors, starting with Kikugoro the First (1717–1783). Onoe Kikugoro the Sixth (1885–1940), an actor of broad scope and a good dancer, experimented with fresh ideas, including those from abroad.

Kinokuniya Bunzaemon   A wealthy merchant from Kii in the middle Edo Period. He made an enormous fortune by daring to carry cargoes of tangerines by boat from Kii to Edo [Tokyo], braving a storm, and also by buying the lumber of Kiso when the Meireki conflagration occurred in Edo.

Kintaro   The childhood name of Kintoki Sakata, one of the four famous retainers of Minamoto-no-Raiko. According to the legend, he was the son of a mountain witch and as a child played with animals such as bears.

kirizansho   Sweetened rice powder cake with ginger

"Kogo"   A composition for the koto, written in the middle of the Edo period, with lyrics by Yokota Taio and music by Yamada Kengyo. According to the *Tale of Heike,* Kogo, the daughter of a high-ranking courtier, waits on and is loved by Emperor Takakura but, at the age of twenty-three, is forced by the powerful regent Taira-no-Kiyomori to become a nun.

"Kojimachi" (#27)   Either an animal or bird appears in every line of this song. "Streetwalker" in the fourth line puns with "a bird called goatsucker" (both *yotaka* in Japanese). The first three lines are intended to introduce the fourth line.

koku   47.654 U.S. gallons

konnyaku   A popular non-caloric gelatinous food made from the root of a bulbous perennial herb and molded into blocks. *Konnyaku* is an ingredient of *oden*. *Shirataki* (*konnyaku* in the shape of fine noodles) is an important ingredient of *sukiyaki*.

kotatsu   An apparatus for warming the body in a Japanese-style room. One type of *kotatsu* probably used in Sawamura-san's household burns charcoal or briquettes in a bowl of ash, which is placed in a clay container shaped like a hut, called *anka*. The *anka* is placed in a square wooden frame with legs. A coverlet *futon* is draped from the frame, and the lower part of the body and the hands are placed within the frame for warmth. Another type of *kotatsu* is a pit cut into the floor, above which the frame is placed. Today an electric heater is the usual source of heat for the *kotatsu*.

koto   A thirteen-stringed, plucked musical instrument made of paulonia wood, about two meters long and shaped like a half-tube

Kyoto doll   A girl's doll with a pageboy hairstyle

– L –

laver   A kind of seaweed, dried and shaped like paper, eaten after roasting

– M –

machi   A town or section of a town

marumage   One of the coiffures of a married woman

Matt-san   When pronounced quickly, "Matsu-san" becomes "Matt-san."

menko   A toy in the form of a circular or rectangular pasteboard with the picture of a favorite children's character on the front. By throwing his *menko* near his opponent's, one child tries to flip over the other's *menko.* If he succeeds, he wins the opponent's piece.

miso   Bean paste, the basic flavoring of Japanese cuisine, together with *shoyu* (soy sauce). *Miso* is made by mixing steamed soybeans with salt and *koji,* a fermenting agent made of rice, wheat, or soy beans.

momoware   In the early part of the twentieth century, the hair style worn by girls in their mid-teens

moxibustion   *Moxa* is a combustible substance derived from *yomogi* [mugwort]. A traditional East Asian medical treatment is to apply cones of moxa on the skin at specific points and ignite them. Some parents threaten to punish their children's bad behavior with it.

mukago   Yam bulbit, a bean-shaped fruit growing on a yam stem

-myojin   An honorific to a deity

– N –

nagahibachi   An oblong brazier, placed in the living room, usually with a kettle boiling. It suggests the seat of the master of the house.

nagauta   A lyrical song accompanied by *shamisen* music, common in Kabuki theater and in concerts. It arose in Kansai but developed in Edo primarily as Kabuki dance music. A *nagauta* ensemble consists of several *shamisen,* singers, hand drums, stick drums, and flutes.

Nakamise   The street leading from the gate of a temple's precincts to the main hall and the shops lining the street. A nakamise can be found in most large temples. The Nakamise of the Senso-ji temple, with shops crowding the side streets too, is well known and, together with the temple, is one of Tokyo's tourist attractions.

Nara   Capital of Japan from 646 to 794 A.D.

night stall *(yomise)*   Night stalls are set up along a street or in the precincts of a temple or shrine when crowds are expected on such occasions as a fair.

Nihyaku-toka   The 210th day from Risshun, or approximately September 2. The mid-season variety of rice plants flowers in early September. Because the frequent seasonal typhoons impair the fertilization of flowering rice plants, this day is regarded as critical for the rice crop.

Niō   The guardian god at a temple gate

norimaki   Vinegared rice rolled in laver

– O –

O-   When attached to a girl's first name, a prefix of endearment, as in "O-tei-chan."

obako   A hairstyle worn by women during mourning in the late Edo period and in later years by old women or widows

obi A long sash worn with the kimono

odenya A shop selling *oden,* a favorite food, particularly in winter, consisting of several ingredients simmered in a pot, and eaten with a splash of broth and a bit of hot mustard. Common ingredients are *konnyaku,* shelled hard-boiled eggs, thick slices of radish, *ganmodoki* (dehydrated tofu mixed with vegetables and deep-fried), and *chikuwa* (a hollow tube of grilled fish paste). Oden is often sold with alcoholic drinks at street stalls specializing in the dish.

Oishi Kuranosuke (1659–1703) Head of the forty-seven warriors of Ako, who revenged their dishonored master. The story, called *Chushingura* (The Loyal Warriors' Tale), is well-known.

Okamisan The wife of the owner of an inn or restaurant, who supervises the employees, male and female, and greets guests as the representative of the house. Her husband does not usually show himself at the front.

Omatsuri Sashichi A Kabuki character, a fireman, nicknamed Omatsuri [festival], probably because he epitomizes the high spirits and energy which characterize a shrine festival. Sashichi loves the geisha Koito, and when a ruse creates entanglements in their relationship, the two Edoites exchange sharp retorts.

Oyoshi the Boa (Uwabami no Oyoshi) A Kabuki character in the play of the same name, whose arm bears a tattoo of a boa and who, by seductive means, revenges herself on Gunjuro, who had killed her husband

(o)zoni A traditional New Year's dish, a soup in which *mochi* [rice cake] is boiled with various ingredients. Rice cake is thought to bring good fortune.

– R –

rikisha   A passenger cart pulled by a man

Risshun   The first day of spring, i.e., New Year's Day of the ancient solar calendar. Risshun falls on February 3 or 4 in the modern calendar.

rokan   A bamboo or ivory tool inserted onto a finger. The player strikes the string of a one- or two- stringed koto with the *rokan* to produce sound.

– S –

saké   Rice liquor

-sama   See "Address, forms of."

-san   See "Address, forms of."

Sanja-sama   The Asakusa Shrine located in the precincts of the Senso-ji temple. During the reign of Empress Suiko (592–628), two fisherman brothers caught an image of Buddha in their net. They, along with the man who protected the image in his home, were enshrined in Sanja-sama as gods by the homeowner's son. The present building was erected in 1649 and is designated as a national treasure.

sashimi   Slices of raw fish, considered a delicacy

satoimo   The taro plant, whose oblong root is edible

sen   One hundredth of a yen

Senso-ji temple   One of the largest in Tokyo, the temple in Asakusa forms the background of Sawamura's recollections. The temple is popularly known as the Asakusa Kannon and was patronized by the Edo government. Senso-ji is known for a number of festivals and events (depicted in chapters six, eleven, seventeen, thirty-three, forty-three, and elsewhere throughout the book). The Denpo-in is the residence of the superior priest.

setsubun   Setsubun originally referred to the eve of the first day of any of the twenty-four divisions of the solar year known as *setsu*. Later it was applied specifically to the last day of the last setsu of the year, called *daikan* (great cold). This day corresponds to the eve of Risshun. Setsubun falls on February 3 or 4 of the Gregorian calendar now used. On Setsubun, soybeans are scattered inside and outside the house with the chant "Out with demons! In with good luck!" Family members customarily eat the same number of beans as their age.

shamisen   A three-stringed plucked lute. The instrument is about a meter long, and the player uses a *bachi* held in the right hand to pluck the strings. Playing the *shamisen* and singing are essential skills required of a geisha. The *shamisen* also accompanies *joruri* chanting in the Bunraku puppet show and *nagauta* chanting in a Kabuki play.

shimada coiffure   A hairstyle for an unmarried woman, as well as for a bride at her wedding. *Yuiwata* is a variety of *shimada*.

Shitamachi   Literally, "low-lying town." The term referred to the eastern part of Edo (Tokyo) along the Sumida River (roughly the current Chuo, Taito, and Sumida Wards) and contrasted to *yamanote* [foothills]. In the Edo period (1603–1868), merchants and artisans lived in Shitamachi, while the *samurai* lived in the Yamanote area. With the increasing vitality of merchants in the middle and late Edo period, Shitamachi blossomed, and the pleasure quarters of Yoshiwara and Asakusa, parts of Shitamachi, prospered. In contrast to the severe standards of warrior society, the townspeople developed a distinctive personality, called *Edokko katagi* (an Edoite's temperament). See "Edokko." With the Meiji Restoration (1868), Edo became Tokyo and has expanded greatly since, resulting in a dilution of *Edokko Katagi*. Yet this temperament is still evident in the area. Sawamura-san's recollections reflect her fondness for the spirit, and she depicts her father as embodying *Edokko Katagi*. *(Adapted from* JIE*)*

sho   0.477 U.S. gallon

shoji   A sliding paper- or glass-fitted screen

Shoki   Chinese mythic being who dispels demons. The pictorial subject of the "demon queller" originated in the Chinese legend of Zhong Bui, the scholar-recluse, who cured the ailing T'ang emperor Xuan-zong by driving away his devil in a dream. Zhong Bui is portrayed wearing a Chinese robe, high boots, and a black scholar's hat. He strikes a threatening pose with bulging eyes, an abundant beard, and a sword in hand. In Japan Shoki first appeared in the twelfth-century *Jigoku-Zoshi* (Scrolls of Hells). He is associated with the Boys' Festival in May, when his image is displayed to overpower evil and pestilence.

soba   Buckwheat noodles

sun   3.3 centimeters, or 1.1193 inches

sushi   A small block of vinegared rice, topped with raw fish

sutra   The sermons of Buddha

– T –

tabi   A sock with a separation between the big toe and other toes to accommodate a thonged sandal or clog. White *tabi* are worn with formal kimono, while solid dark colors are for ordinary occasions. *Tabi* fasten at the ankle with metal clasps.

Takasago   A Noh play written by Zeami. A scene in the play where an old couple clean the ground under a pine tree is well known. The couple, deities of the Takasago Shrine and the Sumiyoshi Shrine, symbolize a long marriage and longevity. A passage from the play is often sung at a wedding ceremony to celebrate the occasion.

tatami   A mat for flooring a Japanese-style room, consisting of a bed of straw, 2.4 inches thick, covered with a soft surface of woven rush. Its long borders are covered with cloth. A *tatami* is about six by three feet, and the space of a room is measured by the number of *tatami* to cover it.

tempura   Deep-fried fish or vegetables

to   4.765 U.S. gallons, equal to ten *sho*

torii   A gate-like structure placed at key points in a Shinto shrine precinct or on a path leading to the shrine. It consists of two columns and two horizontal rails, the first rail placed on the tops of the columns and the second rail, a little below it, penetrating the columns.

tsubo   3.954 square yards

– U –

Utaemon   Nakamura Utaemon, a well-known hereditary name of Kabuki actors, handed down to the present day. Utaemon the Fifth (1865–1940) was primarily an *onnagata* [a female impersonator] and his son, Utaemon the Sixth, is a leading *onnagata* of the contemporary stage.

– Y –

Yakko-no-Koman   One meaning of *yakko* is a "man of chivalry," and geisha Koman was so nicknamed because of her chivalrous spirit.

yatsude   An evergreen shrub of the family *Araliaceae*

yono-buton   A futon with the width of four of the standard units of a roll of cloth (36 centimeters)

Yoshiwara   From the early Edo period (1617) to 1958, the government-regulated center for prostitution, first in Nihonbashi but later (1657) moved near Asakusa, in the neighborhood of the Senso-ji temple

yuiwata   A variety of the shimada coiffure for a girl of nineteen to twenty-one or twenty-two years

yukata   A cotton summer kimono

– Z –

zarusoba   Buckwheat noodles served on a bamboo tray

zori   Thonged sandals